HIDDEN
HISTORY
of
MAYNARD

To Kirsten

David A. Mark

D.A Mark
History is
everywhere!

Charleston — London

THE
History
PRESS

Published by The History Press

Charleston, SC 29403
www.historypress.net

Copyright © 2014 by David A. Mark
All rights reserved

All photos, unless stated otherwise, courtesy of David A. Mark.

First published 2014

Manufactured in the United States

ISBN 978.1.62619.541.7

Library of Congress CIP data applied for.

CONTENTS

Contents

ACKNOWLEDGEMENTS

Much of the content in this book first appeared as "Life Outdoors," a column in Maynard's *Beacon-Villager* newspaper. Over the years, editors Brian Nanos, Bruce Coulter, Caitlyn Kelleher, Joyce Crane and Holly Camero have been willing to let my curiosity lead me to obscure topics not covered by previously published histories of Maynard.

Volunteers of the Maynard Historical Society, through tedious labor, have collected, cataloged, scanned and computerized a vast collection of artifacts, documents and photographs (a job that will always be a work in progress). The opportunity to pull out a box or open a file drawer led to many of the articles and photographs in this book. Their aid extended to rescanning original photos in the MHS collection. Information also came from the historical societies of Acton, Concord, Framingham, Stow and Sudbury. The resources of the Maynard Public Library time and time again helped me find confirmation of tenuously documented facts. Key resources included microfilm of old newspapers, a complete collection of the town's annual reports and the out-of-print histories of Maynard written for the 50th and 100th anniversaries of the creation of the town.

Individuals provided ideas, stories, leads and links to obscure sources. Thanks to Peggy Jo Brown, John Erb, Linda (Coughlan) Flint, Karen Hamilton, Wilma Hanson, Fred Johnson, Jack Mason, Robert Merriam, Jero Nesson, John Savignano and others for their contributions. Special thanks to Merry Morgan Hill of the Morgan family of Worcester. Amory Maynard's granddaughter Lessie married Charles Morgan. Merry is Lessie's great-granddaughter and keeper of family artifacts, which included a transcript of Harlan Maynard's 1857 diary.

Special thanks also to Henry David Thoreau for the writings he left behind.

Commissioning editor Tabitha Dulla, project editor Ben Ellenburg and image editor Gracie Aghapour—all with The History Press— shaped my concepts and my content into this book. Those contributions are deeply appreciated.

My wife, Jean D'Amico, always reads my work before it is submitted to the newspaper. For the writing of my first book, *Maynard: History and Life Outdoors*, and now for this book, she has shown great forbearance in taking on the task of reading everything all over again.

This book is dedicated to family members: those still with us, those gone in body but with us in memory, those who had full lives on this earth and those taken early.

INTRODUCTION

How much history can be written about one small town? This is a valid question, and one I hear often when acquaintances comment on the latest newspaper column. After all, my first book, *Maynard: History and Life Outdoors*, was a collection of close to fifty columns written over two years, and this book is more of the same.

The question becomes even more appropriate when asked not in the context of these two books existing in a historical vacuum but rather against the history—that word again—of there being nearly a dozen other books about Maynard.

The first answer is that history is fractal. For those unfamiliar with the word, a non-mathematical explanation is to think of a town dominated by steep hills and valleys. From five thousand feet above the town, a straight line from one side to the other would be a certain distance. Walking the same line would be longer because of the ups and downs. At ant level, the distance becomes longer still.

The analogy for history is to find small topics. So, no history of the mill per se, or the famous few, but rather: Where were the bricks made? How much water power was generated by the river? Were the residents drinkers or abstainers? Did anyone shoot rats at the town dump? (Cambridge, fifty horsepower, both, yes.)

The second answer is that history is never-ending. Many history books look way, way back and, by doing so, neglect the recent past. This book finishes with a chapter on the early twenty-first century, because if not captured now, then when? Who will remember that Maynard was host to Monster.com? Or how ArtSpace got started?

Millions of bricks constituting the older mill buildings are thought to have come from the New England Brick Company in Cambridge, Massachusetts. Nathaniel Wyeth owned brickworks there and also built a brick ice house on the west side of the millpond in 1849. He may have been partially responsible for Irish brickmakers and ice cutters settling in what would become Maynard to take jobs in the new woolen mill.

And then: "Hidden History." The title's theme is the publisher's choice for a series of books about various local histories, but interpretation is left to the individual authors. Should that mean dark history, full of crimes, sins and corruption? Or secret history—the sort investigated by Indiana Jones and his ilk? Perhaps neglected history? By shining a light on the last, this collection tries to go where other recountings have not tread.

The last silo in Maynard, photographed in 2014, is a reminder that even though Maynard was very much a mill town, it once was also home to 350 milk cows (per 1890 tax records).

ONLY IN MAYNARD

Maynard is different from neighboring towns. Firstly, it is much smaller in area. Secondly, its founding as a named town came one to two centuries later than that of its neighbors. And thirdly, the people are different, and have always been different.

"Only in Maynard"

Ten years ago, it was possible to buy "Only in Maynard" bumper stickers, T-shirts and sweatshirts at local stores and at Maynard Fest. Lettering was orange against a black background—Maynard's school colors. The sole remnant of this endeavor is bumper stickers for sale at Russell's.

"Only in..." can have different meanings: "Only in Vegas" has one, and the "Only in Portland" ethos of the cable TV show *Portlandia*, another entirely. *Only in America* was a TV show about taking pride in things American, while "Only in Boulder" is the motto of www.keepboulderweird.org. (Life in Boulder includes the Naked Pumpkin Run: flash mobs of people running down streets wearing real or plastic jack-o'-lanterns on their heads—and nothing else, except running shoes.)

"Only in Maynard" was deliberately printed so that the right side was noticeably higher than the left. Best guess is the wording was askew to convey that negative, rueful pride that only in Maynard could things (such as town things, school things, people things) be so humorously incompetent or fouled up.

"Only in Maynard" bumper sticker. The design is orange text on black.

An example: the use of snow blowers on the roof of Memorial Gym during the big-snow winter of 2010–11 was intended to save the roof from risk of collapse but instead resulted in roof damage, leading to leaks and severe water damage to the gym floor, which had been completely refurbished only months before. In the end, this contributed one more reason for demolition of the gym in 2012. The site is now a parking lot for ArtSpace.

Back in 2005, to counter the prevailing negative impression, a group of civic-minded citizens approached the editor of the *Beacon-Villager* to see if they could take turns writing a pro-Maynard column featuring the friendly and welcoming nature of this unique small town. The column lasted only a few months. Only in Maynard.

An echo of that positive intent was conveyed in a 2008 article in the newspaper that read, in part, "A clever slogan, coined some few years ago, continues to describe our singular uniqueness, our melting pot citizenry and our basic values for the 'good life.' That slogan, 'Only in Maynard,' sets up the town as a special place where very special people do distinctive and exceptional things. This is especially true in the art of song and music as developed in our town."

An informal survey of people about town yielded both the negative and positive connotations and also a third meaning: the concept of specialness. Only in Maynard can you see Santa Claus arriving by helicopter for the Christmas parade. Only in Maynard can you still find a local movie theater. Only in Maynard are the bars close enough together to have a pub crawl that might involve actual crawling (or at least walking) rather than driving.

Harking back to the origin, the bumper stickers have "TM" superscripted above the end of "Only in Maynard," signifying that an application had been filed for a trademark. An initial check of the records of the U.S. Patent and Trademark Office found that no application was ever filed, the omission apparently qualifying as one more "Only in Maynard" example. However, further research found that a state-only service mark was in fact approved by the Commonwealth of Massachusetts in September 2003.

So after all this debate, what does "Only in Maynard" really mean today? Whether it is only in this small town that people are so warm, friendly and welcoming; or only here that things are so ruefully, headshakingly messed up; or a comment on the unique nature of life in Maynard, my own opinion is that, in comparison, bumper stickers reading "Only in Acton" or "Only in Sudbury" would make no sense whatsoever.

How Maynard Became Maynard

Maynard was carved out of Sudbury and Stow in April 1871, which explains why it is so much newer than those towns, which were founded in 1639 and 1683, respectively. Before 1871, everything north of the Assabet River was part of Stow and south of the river, part of Sudbury. Maynard's boundary consists of five straight lines forming a five-sided polygon, 8.27 miles total length, surrounding a land area of 5.40 square miles. Massachusetts State Acts of 1871, Chapter 198, describes in detail how the lines were drawn:

> *All the territory now within the towns of Stow and Sudbury comprised within the following limits, that is to say—Beginning at the northwesterly corner of said territory, at the northwesterly corner bound of land of the late Daniel Whitney, and the town line between Acton and Stow; thence southerly in a straight line to a stake and stones at the northeasterly corner of land of William Carr, at land of Benjamin Smith on the top of Carr's Hill, so called; thence southeasterly in a straight line to a stone monument in the town line between Stow and Sudbury, at land of Winthrop Puffer; thence easterly in a straight line to the guidepost at the Iron Works causeway, so called; thence northerly to a stone monument at the corner of Action and Concord town lines, in the Sudbury town line; thence northwesterly by the town line of Acton and Sudbury and Acton and Stow town line to the point of beginning, is hereby incorporated into a town by the name of Maynard.*
>
> *—Approved April 19, 1871*

Daniel Whitney and his wife, Sarah (Marble) Whitney, lived on a farm on the border of what had been the Stow–Acton boundary, but shortly after his death, it became the Maynard–Acton boundary. Sarah was fifth-generation Marble family at this site, from 1710 onward. Daniel's family had been in Stow for five generations before he married Sarah.

Those details can be put into present-day context. It was "the late Daniel Whitney" because he had died in 1870. His farmland extended northwest from what is now Route 27, along what was then the Acton–Stow border. This northernmost stone marker is deep in the woods north of the end of Rockland Avenue.

Heading southwest, the next corner is on the hilltop in the apple orchard bordering the north side of Maynard's Summer Street. Benjamin Smith (for whom the Ben Smith Dam is named) had strong family connections in Assabet Village. His land ended up in Maynard, while Carr, his neighbor, opted to remain in Stow. The south-heading line went to the Puffer family farm. This marker is in the Assabet River National Wildlife Refuge. The eastward line crosses Puffer Pond to end at a stone marker adjacent to Route 27. The northeastward line ends at a point just off Sudbury Road, about a third of a mile south of where Sudbury Road meets Powder Mill Road.

The northeast border was the preexisting border between the town of Acton and the towns of Sudbury and Stow, established in 1735, when Acton separated from Concord. In fact, there is a line marker just north of the Assabet River, with an "A" on one side and an "S" (for Stow) on the other, because its placement predates the founding of Maynard. The other lines were new creations. Maynard started with a population of about eight hundred people from Stow and nine hundred people from Sudbury.

A 1904 atlas of boundaries of towns in Middlesex Country provided longitude and latitude for each of the five corners, a description of location relative to then-current landmarks—some long since gone—and physical descriptions of stone markers erected at each corner. Recent visits confirmed four of the five markers are exactly as described in the atlas. The southernmost stone was replaced by the U.S. Army in 1942 with a granite block embedded flush to the ground. The base of the original stone lies on

Granite posts were installed at each corner. This one, at the point touched by Maynard, Sudbury, Concord and Acton, indicates when representatives of town governments checked the boundaries to confirm that neighboring towns were not encroaching. The order of letters on the four faces of the stone (M-C-A-S) does not match the true order (M-S-C-A).

the ground a few feet away. The top of the original stone, inscribed with the appropriate letters, is in the possession of the Maynard Historical Society.

On May 21, 2011, Maynard's town officials and historical society members "perambulated the bounds" (well, maybe not every foot) and painted "2011" on the existing stone markers. This task is supposed to be performed every five years. Maynard has missed many visits. Acton, Concord, Stow and Sudbury have been more diligent.

Petitions for a Greater Maynard

How Maynard's boundaries were set is an interesting question. There were some exploratory town-founding rumblings in 1869 and 1870. In an undated petition with sixty-eight signatures—never submitted to the state— the name of the proposed town was left blank. That petition proposed to take land from four towns: Acton, Concord, Sudbury and Stow, and lists the gunpowder mill along with the paper mill and cotton and wool mill.

Maynard Historical Society president David Griffin and board of trustees member Paul Boothroyd accept the donation of the initial petition to form a new town out of parts of Sudbury, Stow, Acton and Concord.

The official petition to the Commonwealth of Massachusetts, proposing to take land only from Sudbury and Stow, was signed by seventy-one men and dated January 26, 1871. While some town histories refer to only this list as the founders of Maynard, three subsequent supportive petitions with sixty-three additional signers were submitted in January and February. Add the names appended to the unsubmitted petition and collectively nearly two hundred signatures were gathered (there were a few duplications). Among the signatories were men associated with each of the three mills: Nathan Pratt, William Parker and Lorenzo Maynard. Interestingly, Amory Maynard's signature does not appear on any of the petitions.

Key points of the complaint were that the fast-growing population clustered around the mills on the Assabet River were miles away from the town centers of Sudbury and Stow and were not getting adequate school and street improvement spending despite taxes being paid to the parent towns.

The official petition's proposed borders were not the same as what was approved a few months later. What was proposed was much larger—a Greater Maynard. The following description from the January petition starts at what is currently the northern corner of Maynard and works its way counterclockwise back to the starting point:

> *Beginning at the North West corner of the farm of the late Daniel Whitney, thence running Southerly to the road Westerly of the house of Jonathan P. Bent; thence more easterly on a straight line to the town line separating Stow from Hudson; thence Easterly on said line town line to the South East corner of Stow; thence North Easterly on a straight line crossing Bottomless and Willis' Pond to the Concord town line, at or near the place familiarly known as Dungee Hole; thence North Westerly on said town line of Concord & on the town line of Acton to the point of beginning.*

The vague part of the description is determining where the proposed borderline would reach the Concord town line, as there is no current map showing Bottomless Pond nor a place "familiarly known as Dungee Hole." However, we know the former became Crystal Pond, and Henry David Thoreau's *Journal* mentions "Dunge Hole" as a hollow near Concord's White Pond. A Concord map, dating from 1906, has Dunge Hole Brook as close to where Route 117 crosses the Concord-Sudbury border. Looking at a map, a straight line can indeed be drawn from the southeast corner of Stow to the Concord border at Route 117, bisecting both ponds on the way. One theory is that the proposed southeast border was chosen to align with the southeast border of the "two-mile grant" that extended Sudbury northwest to the Assabet River in 1649.

The net result of these proposed borders would have been A) a bit more land left to Stow on the northeast border; B) Maynard getting a larger piece of southeast Stow; and C) a much larger part of north Sudbury going to Maynard. This Greater Maynard, even without taking any land from Acton or Concord, would still have been nearly twice the town's present-day size.

To Be or Not to Be?

There was opposition to the petition. Stow residents countered with three remonstrances, or petitions against, stating, among other things, that such a division would remove "the only portion that has increased in its population and in its valuation for the past ten years" and also that such a sundering "would leave our ancient town in a weak and crippled condition to which we most decidedly object." The remonstrances were signed by a total of 160 of Stow's residents.

On January 23, 1871, Sudbury residents voted 183 to 88 against allowing part of the town to split off and formed a committee "to use all honorable means which in their judgment will aid in preventing the formation of a new town." After the fact, the same committee was assigned to get the best financial settlement.

Maynard prevailed, but with compromises. The way Paul Boothroyd, well-known Maynard history buff, puts it, "The Brigham brothers and Webster Cutting wanted to be part of the new town, but Sudbury hired the surveyors who drew the final, smaller border." As indirect support of this theory, Sudbury's town meeting record from April 1872 states, "We have attended to making a survey and establishing a line between said towns…We have also erected stone monuments marked S. & M. at such places as said line crosses the highways."

A visit was made to the Commonwealth of Massachusetts Archives in an attempt to find official documents pertaining to the boundary lines dispute. A collection of original documents referred to as Legislative Packet 1871, Chapter 198, contained the four petitions in support of the proposed formation of Maynard, the three remonstrances from Stow residents opposing the action and the bill dated April 19, 1871, approving the action with the finalized—i.e., present-day—boundary lines. There was no documentation in the Chapter 198 packet to shed light on the changes from the petition to the final boundary lines.

Thus, Maynard was founded on Patriots' Day 1871, twenty-four years after the founding of the carpet mill. According to the book *History of Maynard, 1871–1891*, the new name was chosen to honor mill-founder Amory Maynard by unanimous vote of the citizens. However, it is not entirely clear when this "vote" was taken, as the official petition had already stipulated that the new town bear the name Maynard.

The Price of Becoming a Town

The towns losing land agreed to accept payments. Stow received $6,500 plus interest (totaling $1,470) spread out over seven years. Sudbury received $20,883.28 initially, plus $2,700 as $300 per year over nine years, for support of the poor. Sudbury got more than Stow because the wool and paper mills and railroad were in Sudbury and because the initial payment included $10,400 for 104 shares of town-owned stock in the Fitchburg Railroad. Payment documentation is in Maynard's early annual reports, with the 1880–81 annual report confirming the final payment to Sudbury. To put these payments in context, a female teacher's salary was $360 per year, and a man's pay for road building was $1.75 per day.

Maynard threw a big party to celebrate its formation. How is this known? Because the treasurer's report in the first annual report itemizes, among other costs, $34.13 for fireworks, $30.00 for a band, $32.65 for "use of cannons" and $14.00 for three kegs of gunpowder.

Interestingly, Sudbury's town meeting records from April 1872 show that the Town of Maynard went through a bit of buyer's remorse. Maynard, it appears, petitioned the state legislature to "relieve them from a fulfillment of their obligations to the town of Sudbury." As Maynard had already paid the $20,883.28 on October 6, 1871, this could mean only that Maynard wanted out of the remaining $2,700 to be paid out over nine years. Sudbury's representatives opposed the petition before the state legislature, which ruled in their favor.

Consequences of the schism included smaller populations in Stow and Sudbury. According to the 1871 census for Maynard, the newly minted town started with a population 1,820. This was larger than what was left behind in each of the parent towns. Not only that, but Stow and

The Fitchburg Railroad reached Amory Maynard's woolen mill in 1849 as a spur off the Boston-to-Fitchburg line. In 2014, the last of the rails were removed in preparation for construction of the Assabet River Rail Trail; no trains had run on them for fifty years. A common practice was to hammer date nails into wooden ties to signify when last replaced. This photo shows a date nail from 1936, found on the rail bed behind Nason Street.

Sudbury stayed close to their post-succession populations for decades, while Maynard continued to grow. For at least seventy-five years after the formation of Maynard, its population continued to be larger than the populations of Stow and Sudbury combined.

2

MEET THE MAYNARD FAMILY

G iven the town was named after Amory Maynard while he was still alive, there is remarkably little knowledge or presence of the man today—no biography, no statue, no school, no park. There is a family crypt and a clock tower (built by his son), but more on those anon. Amory was not running a benevolent company town. The Assabet Manufacturing Company had rules for employees. According to an 1863 poster reprinted in the book *Assabet Mills*, employees were expected to keep the Sabbath, observe all regulations and be temperate, skillful and honest. Quitting workers had to give two weeks' notice in order to get their last paychecks but could be fired without notice. There was a 9:00 p.m. curfew, after which workers were expected to be off the streets.

Ancestors and Descendants

In 1846, at the age of forty-two, Amory Maynard moved his wife and three sons to a house in the sparsely settled Assabet River Valley so he and his partner, William H. Knight, could dam the Assabet River and build a mill. They started with carpets—in time adding blankets and wool cloth for suits and dresses. Part of their good luck was already being in wool goods when the Civil War embargo cut off Northern cotton mills from access to Southern cotton.

Looking in the ancestral direction, Amory was six generations away from John Maynard, who had decided to leave England for the colonies. He and

Amory Maynard, seventh generation in Massachusetts, bought hundreds of acres of land and water rights to the Assabet River to start a woolen mill. *Courtesy of Maynard Historical Society.*

his young son, also named John, transited the Atlantic, year and ship unknown, but by 1638 were among the initial settlers of Sudbury.

As with almost all of the genealogy of early colonial families, research is hindered by the frequency of second marriages and shortage of distinguishing names. For example, there are two John Maynard colonists from England, both born around 1598 and both marrying women named Mary. Neither was related to two non-emigrating John Maynards, same era, who were knights in England and who coincidentally both married women named Mary.

Our John Maynard lived in Sudbury. His son John, by his first marriage, married twice and had either nine or eleven children. Next in line, Simon, married only once, but he and his wife, Hannah, had ten children. Their son Ephriam married twice and had nine children. Ephriam's uncle Ephriam had fifteen children by three wives. Isaac Maynard had only two children, of whom the older was our Amory.

All this descending raises the question—are there any of Amory Maynard's descendants alive today? Of Amory's sons, Harlan died young. Lorenzo had five children, none with living issue. William had seven children. William's daughter Lessie Louise Maynard married Paul Beagary Morgan, of the wealthy and well-known Morgan family of Worcester. Lessie and Paul had five children, who begat children of their own, so there are a scattering of Amory's descendants in Massachusetts. Another line descends from William's son, Harlan James Maynard. Anne Bancroft traces back from present-day through her mother, Nancy Jane Maynard, to Harlan Junior and thence to Harlan. This makes her a great-great-great-granddaughter of Amory.

Table I
AMORY MAYNARD'S ANCESTORS

John Maynard	1598–1672	Elizabeth Ashton/Mary Axtell
John Maynard	1630–1711	Mary Gates/Sarah Keyes
Simon Maynard	1666–1748	Hannah Newton
Ephriam Maynard	1707–????	Sarah Livermore/Mary Balcom
Simon Maynard	1748–1818	Silence Priest
Isaac Maynard	1779–1820	Lydia Howe
Amory Maynard	1804–1890	Mary Priest
Lorenzo Maynard	1829–1904	Lucy Ann Davidson
William Maynard	1833–1906	Mary Adams
Harlan Maynard	1843–1861	did not marry

Given the large families of many of the early colonists, it will be no surprise that our original immigrant had other descendants of note. Edward Maynard (b. 1813) was a military inventor who improved greatly on the mechanics of the breech-loading rifle. Charles Johnson Maynard (b. 1845) was a well-known Massachusetts naturalist. Hannah, a granddaughter of the first John Maynard, married Jonathan Davenport. Three generations later, Hannah's great-granddaughter married Captain Timothy Bush, a veteran of the French and Indian War of 1756. And six generations later, we arrive at George H.W. Bush, forty-first president of the United States!

The Family, Warts and All

Highlights of juicy family stories: Lorenzo married the housemaid just after her sixteenth birthday; William married the girl next door when he was twenty and she twenty-two (their first child arrived three months later); teenage Harlan begged his brother to get him a job in Boston (in a letter, he wrote, "I am sick of Assabet, I want to leave"). When Amory retired from the mill, Lorenzo became agent (equivalent to today's title of chief operating officer), and Lorenzo's son was promoted to superintendent over his uncle William, who, perhaps stewing in disappointment, moved his family to California. The mill went bankrupt in 1898. Lorenzo was accused of protecting his own investments at the expense

Table II
AMORY MAYNARD'S CHILDREN AND GRANDCHILDREN

Amory Maynard	1804–1890
married Mary Priest	1805–1886
Lorenzo Maynard	1829–1904
married Lucy Davidson	1833–1903
William H.	1851–1925
Frances (Fanny)	1853–1889
Mary L.	1857–1878
Victoria	1859–1861
Hattie	1864–1885
William Maynard	1833–1906
married Mary Adams	1831–1920
Mary Susan	1853–1924
Amory (Amory II)	1855–1928
Jeanette Cherry	1860–1939
Lessie Louise	1868–1940
Harlan James	1870–1939
Grace Ella	1873–????
George Elmer	1873–1901
Harlan Maynard	1843–1861

of employee savings. He relocated to Winchester. Maynard almost voted to rename itself Assabet. A few months after Lorenzo's death and interment in the family crypt in Maynard, he and his family's remains were transferred to a much fancier mausoleum at Mount Auburn Cemetery. When Lorenzo's son died, he specified that nothing was to go to any of his cousins, even though he had no other heirs. They contested in court and lost. Whew!

The September 1850 census listed Amory Maynard as the head of a Sudbury two-unit household of twenty-four people that included his family, the Adams family, servants and millworkers. Lorenzo was twenty-one; Lucy Ann Davidson, the house servant, was sixteen. They married in October, after she turned seventeen, and they had their first child thirteen months later. William married Mary Adams in July 1853, and their first child, Mary Susan, was born three months later. Both marriages lasted more than fifty years and together produced twelve children, but nine of those died without having surviving children of their own.

Harlan Maynard, the third son, died at age eighteen—one source specified typhoid fever. Letters in the possession of the Morgan family (descendants of his brother William) portray a spirited young man who was frustrated with small-town life; Assabet Village, as it was known then, had only a few hundred residents. As a teenager, Harlan commuted by train to a private school in Concord, where his classmates included Ralph Waldo Emerson's son.

William had a lesser role in the mill's business affairs than older brother Lorenzo. In the 1860s, he lived in Boston for a while and worked for the Fitchburg Railroad. Tax records from 1871 find him back in Maynard and show Amory, Lorenzo and William with incomes of $9,000, $4,000 and $800, respectively. The combined landownership of the mill, the A&L Maynard Company (a real estate and construction business) and Amory's personal holdings came to 270 acres.

Ten years later, Amory owned a mansion on Beechmont Avenue (now Dartmouth Street), extensive landholdings and cash assets of $65,000. Lorenzo also owned a mansion (still standing at 5–7 Dartmouth, stained-glass windows intact) and cash assets of $35,000, while William, at age forty-nine, married and with seven children, was living in a house owned by his father.

Amory Maynard stepped down as mill agent in 1885, shortly after having suffered a stroke. Lorenzo was promoted from superintendent to agent. Lorenzo's son, William H. Maynard, became superintendent. Although Amory was the largest shareholder, the post-bankruptcy financial reorganization of the Assabet Manufacturing Company in 1862 had resulted in T.A. Goddard becoming president of the company.

At about the time of Amory's retirement in 1885, his son William moved himself, his wife and the five youngest of his seven children first to Pasadena and then to Los Angeles—at the time a smallish city of twenty-five thousand people. Married daughter Mary Susan and married son Amory both remained in Maynard. Historical accounts state that the move was for William's health—nature of illness unstated. It is plausible he had tuberculosis, as moving to a hot, dry climate was that era's treatment of choice. But it is also a bit interesting that he moved in the year his brother took over the mill. Regardless, three years later, he was well enough to relocate east but chose Worcester over returning to Maynard.

Amory Maynard's death left Lorenzo and William wealthy men. Amory died without leaving a will. Lorenzo was made administrator of the estate, charged with tallying up the net worth, collecting money owed and settling all debts. Although the probate records are silent on the distribution, a good guess is that the estate was divided equally between the two brothers.

Mary (Adams) Maynard, wife of William, daughter-in-law of Amory. Mary and her husband were buried in Hope Cemetery, Worcester. *Courtesy of Morgan family.*

Unfortunately, neither the probate file nor the state archives have any record of an inventory of Amory Maynard's property or net worth at the time of his death.

Lorenzo continued as agent of the mill and Maynard resident. He personally paid for construction of the clock tower in 1892. William continued to live in Worcester until his death in 1906. At about the same time as the clock tower construction, Lorenzo also paid for the chapel addition and the installation of over a dozen stained-glass windows in the Union Congregational Church, a place of worship that his father had been instrumental in getting built in 1853. Six of the windows were dedicated to Lorenzo's parents and to his deceased daughters.

For complex reasons, including an end of federal protective tariffs in the 1890s, the mill failed in late 1898. It was purchased in 1899 by the American Woolen Company. Lorenzo and his son either resigned or were fired, and then William's son Amory was put in charge as agent. Amory was living in what had been his parents' house near the corner of Main and Nason Streets (where CVS is now).

Lorenzo moved to Winchester, where he died in March 1904, a millionaire at a time when an average worker's wages were $500 per year. His son William H. Maynard was his sole surviving heir. An October 1904 newspaper article noted that Lorenzo and five other deceased family members were relocated to a new mausoleum in the Mount Auburn Cemetery in Cambridge—a place where all the "best" people were being buried. Correspondence on file at Mount Auburn confirms that Lorenzo bought the plot, #6111, on Crystal Avenue, in April 1903 and immediately ordered the construction of a large mausoleum designed by the renowned Van Amringe Granite Company.

The impressive structure is made of granite, twenty-four feet tall, and had five stained-glass windows (one has since been destroyed). It was completed

Acrimony about the failure of the woolen mill led Lorenzo Maynard to not only move out of town but also contract for an impressive mausoleum in Mount Auburn Cemetery, in Cambridge, and have his deceased family members relocated.

in September 1904. Contributing causes for the postmortem move were bad feelings left over from being displaced at the mill, plus the 1902 effort to change the town's name to Assabet.

When Lorenzo's son died in Winchester in 1925, he left no money to his twelve cousins, even though his wife had died years earlier and they had had no children. Instead, his estate of nearly $1 million was divided among his sister-in-law and twenty-three charities, mostly in Winchester. Harlan J. Maynard, a first cousin, challenged the will in court.

Per an account in the *Winchester Star*, William H. Maynard was described by the lawyer representing the cousins as "a man of secret habits and had few friends, but scores of enemies." Claims were made that he was not of sound mind but rather suffered from "a mental affliction that was inherited through three generations" and that he "thought his servants were trying to poison him." The judge threw all of this out of court.

Amory Maynard, grandson of Amory Maynard, was the last descendant with the family name to live in Maynard. He moved to Cambridge in 1926 and died in 1928. On a mysterious note, his father's will had left money to everyone in the family—except Amory. Mary Susan, his older sister, had four daughters, one of whom, Mary Augusta Peters, married Frank Sanderson. She died in 1947—the last Maynard descendant to live in Maynard. Between deaths and daughters, the family name vanished. There are differently surnamed living descendants via Lessie Louise and Harlan James, but none here.

William H. Knight: The Silent Partner

William H. Knight put more money into the partnership back in 1846, so why aren't we living in the town of Knightsville instead of Maynard? One town wit somewhat disparagingly said that when William Knight and Amory Maynard met, Knight had the money and Maynard had the experience, but by the time their partnership ended, Maynard had the money and Knight had had the experience. The truth was more complex.

In the late eighteenth century, Calvin Maynard constructed a gristmill on Fort Meadow Brook in Marlborough. The grist (grain) mill was soon converted to a sawmill, and its operation was eventually passed on to a relative—Isaac Maynard—whose death in 1820 left his young son Amory in charge. Amory, in addition to operating the mill, expanded into the construction business. He employed as many as fifty men. One of Amory's clients was mill owner William H. Knight, for whom he built the New England Carpet Mill in the Saxonville section of Framingham.

Knight arrived on these shores from England in 1824 at age thirty-two. He was an experienced mechanic with skills in water power and textile machines. He started as a mill superintendent in Framingham; then moved to Tariffville, Connecticut, to partner in a carpet mill; but soon relocated back to Framingham. There he married Elizabeth Stone and started his own mill in 1829 in Saxonville.

Knight's initial successes were modest. He and Elizabeth lived in rooms in the upper story of the factory, overlooking the millpond. Accounts had it that Elizabeth would sometimes fish from their windows to catch their dinner. But by 1845, Knight's operations had expanded to three mill buildings and 232 employees.

Sometime around 1846, the City of Boston purchased the land, dam and water rights to Fort Meadow Pond from Amory Maynard. The amount paid is disputed—various website-posted accounts say as little as $21,000 to as much as $60,000. Even at the low end of that range, Maynard, at age forty-two, was a wealthy man. At the same time, Boston also purchased Knight's mills and water rights to Lake Cochituate (Long Pond). Knight received $150,000; the largest sum that had ever been paid by the City of Boston for water rights up to that time.

In 1846, the two men agreed to partner in a new mill operation on the Assabet River. They started buying land and water rights, including Asa Smith's mill on Mill Street and riverfront land from Ben Smith as a site for the dam. Maynard later bought land around Boon Pond, to be dammed to form a larger body of water, renamed Boon Lake, and

William H. Knight is better remembered in Framingham than in Maynard. *Courtesy Framingham Historical Commission.*

also repurchased Fort Meadow Reservoir from the City of Boston. These upstream assets guaranteed a year-round water supply to power the mill.

Knight and Maynard completed a wood-framed, three-story, fifty- by one-hundred-foot building, which they named Assabet Mills. The new yarn- and carpet-making operation prospered. By 1852, two more wood-framed buildings had been added. Together, the owners donated land for the site of the Union Congregational Church.

For all this, William Knight left little mark on history. He arrived alone with origins unknown but was experienced and ambitious. He went from hired mill superintendent to partner to owning a mill complex in just five years. Although already very wealthy from the water rights buyout, he entered the new venture when he was fifty-four years old.

Knight retired in 1852, at age sixty, just six years after cofounding Assabet Mills with Amory Maynard. It's possible he lost interest in day-to-day operations after the death of his wife in September of that year. They may have never lived in what was then a crude hamlet on a rocky river. One record has Knight moving to Boston in 1848 (downtown Boston initially and then, later, an impressive town house on Walnut Street, Beacon Hill). Pure speculation, but it is possible that Knight ran the in-city business office for the company, communicating with Amory by telegraph. William and Elizabeth had no children. History notes that he died in Boston in 1870 at age seventy-seven, heirs unknown, burial site unknown. *Sic transit gloria mundi.* (Thus passes worldly glory.)

A Boy's Diary, by Amory Maynard's Teenage Son

Friday, October 16, 1857: First, my resolutions. I commence this journal with the resolution that I will write it through in as neat and good a manner as I can. I intend to write some in this book every night. This is my birthday. I am fourteen years old today. I have lived fourteen years of my life very easy, but now I intend to earn my bread by my hands. I went to school to Concord all day, went down in the morning train and came home in the night train. As I am going to record all the important events that come under my observation, I will write a circumstance which I beheld with my own eyes. As the five o'clock train was leaving Acton this evening a man tried to get on after they had started, he missed his step and fell under the hind car and had his arm ground off. No other important events happened today that I know of. The weather has been very dull. Most of the day, it rained.

So begins the first entry in the diary of Harlan Priest Maynard, age fourteen, the third son of Amory and Mary (Priest) Maynard. Harlan continued to make entries on and off through November 15, 1858. The Maynard Historical Society has a copy of a typed transcript created by one of Amory's descendants in 1936.

The Concord school Harlan mentioned attending was a private, coeducational school established by Frank B. Sanborn, a Harvard graduate later famous for his abolitionist activities. Harlan's classmates included Edith and Edward Emerson, children of Ralph Waldo Emerson.

Harlan was living with his parents at 145 Main Street, in what was then informally called Assabet Village. Harlan's diary entries deal mostly with school, attending church services and religious meetings and his chores. School included math, grammar, geography, French, Latin and philosophy. He wrote of chopping wood, tending the family vegetable garden, carrying squashes to the attic for winter storage and so on.

Curiously little was written about the family business. In passing, Harlan mentioned helping his older brothers Lorenzo and William cover rolls in the mill or opening bales of wool. Each bale would have weighed 200 to 450 pounds. On November 14, 1857, he wrote, "The mill is stopped entirely for the big wheel is broke."

Both of his older brothers were married at the time Harlan began his diary. On Christmas Eve 1857, he mentions visiting their houses to help put presents into the children's Christmas stockings.

One surprising piece of information was how often his father was traveling. He was visiting New York or Philadelphia on almost a monthly basis, going into Boston often and at times heading north to New Hampshire. Autumn of that year saw the beginnings of a national depression, later named the Panic of 1857, which lasted into 1859. Overly optimistic business loans to railroads and midwestern farmers had extended the banks. A chain of railroad bankruptcies, bank failures, dropping land values and deflation resulted in massive business cutbacks and unemployment. One of Amory's letters to his family tells of a riot of twenty-five thousand unemployed people that started with a rally in Tompkins Square Park, New York, with the militia called out after the protest turned violent. Mr. Maynard might have been traveling to deal with creditors or seek new investors in the mill, as the accepted history is that the mill was in financial difficulty in 1857, if not actually bankrupt. Yet Harlan's diary clearly suggests there was still some activity throughout 1857 and 1858.

Harlan Maynard died in 1861, at the age of eighteen, of a cause not stated in any of the written histories, but a descendant of his older brother William says Harlan died from typhoid. He was buried in the Glenwood Cemetery but later disinterred, to be placed in the Maynard family crypt, constructed in 1880. His brother William named one of his sons Harlan James Maynard. It is through this Harlan that the family line descends to Bancroft family members.

Where Did the Wool Come From?

The Assabet wool mill morphed into the Assabet Manufacturing Company, in turn bought out and rebirthed as a part of the American Woolen Company. With only brief interruptions, this was a wool-processing town for 103 years (1847–1950). The population grew. Immigrants arrived. There were churches, schools and cemeteries, as well as a train station, taverns, a government and a fire station, all powered by wool. So where did the wool come from?

The first sheep arrived in New England with the colonists but were not of particularly good breeding. Yield was on the order of one pound of wool a year (versus today's ten pounds). Only after the importation of Merino sheep from Spain, starting around 1811, did wool become a serious industry in North America. Napoleon Bonaparte was the catalyst. His invasion of Spain as part of the Peninsular War had as a consequence the export of Merino sheep to England, Canada and the United States—because Spain wanted its then ally, England, to have sources of high-quality wool. Previously, Spain had so protected its wool industry that the crime of smuggling Merinos out of the country was punishable by death.

Ten years later, as a result of vigorous lobbying efforts, the U.S. government enacted the Tariff Act of 1823. This included charging a tariff on foreign wool and wool clothing, in order to both raise revenue and protect its nascent wool industry. By 1840, the states of Maine, New Hampshire and Vermont had more sheep than people. The count for Vermont was 1,682,000 sheep to 292,000 people. Most of the land dedicated to sheep grazing has been marginal hill farms vacated by people either moving west or relocating to cities for factory work. All of New England was crisscrossed with stone fences and sheep pastures. We find the mossy remnants of these stone fences in New England's woods.

Raising sheep meant killing all the wolves. The process started early—the Massachusetts Bay Colony established a bounty on wolves in 1630. The last recorded wolf kill in New England was in Maine in 1893.

Shearing sheep is a hot, dirty job. Traditionally, late spring is when the herds are brought in. Mechanically powered shears are used to remove fleece at two to three minutes per sheep. Fleece are hot-washed, dried and compressed into bales weighing 200 to 450 pounds each for transport, or the wash and dry steps are skipped and wool is baled and shipped "in the grease" (meaning the lanolin and dirt have not been entirely removed). Either way, bales are shipped all over the world. At the dawn of the twenty-

Millworkers waiting by a platform in front of Railroad Street, prepared to load wool onto a train. Photo taken 1920. The buildings behind them still exist. *Courtesy of Maynard Historical Society.*

first century, Australia, China and New Zealand were the top three wool-producing countries.

The value of wool depends on fiber fineness and length. Long fibers with narrow diameter are used for fine-quality clothing, whereas shorter, thicker fibers are used in wool carpets and blankets. We know that, at least initially, Amory Maynard and William Knight's mill was buying and processing wool of poor quality because it was producing only carpets. Over time, its output evolved to include blankets and then woven material for clothing.

To recap, for the first few years of our mill's existence, wool was either sourced locally or brought by train to the South Action train station, where it was off-loaded into horse-drawn wagons for the final two miles of travel. From 1850 onward, Assabet Village had railroad tracks directly to the mill and was probably buying wool from northern states. Maynard family letters in the historical society collection mention Amory's trips to New Hampshire and Maine. Over subsequent decades, sources shifted first to Montana and Idaho and finally to South America, Australia and New Zealand.

Who Is in the Maynard Crypt?

According to documents in the collection of the Maynard Historical Society, the remains of twenty-two people are interred in the Maynard family crypt. Surprisingly, this includes but one of Amory and Mary Maynard's three children and only one of their twelve grandchildren.

The crypt, located on the north side of Glenwood Cemetery, is an imposing earth-covered mound with a granite façade facing the road. The mound is ninety feet across and about twelve feet tall. The stonework façade is thirty feet across. The ceiling of the crypt has a glass skylight surmounted by an exterior cone of iron grillwork. "MAYNARD" graces a granite lintel above the entrance. The six-foot-tall double doors are intricately carved marble. A locked chain secures the doors, but the left door is cracked and partially off its hinges.

Inside, there are eight vaults, three each on the left and right sides and two across the back. Each vault was designed to hold three caskets. Above the three on the left is "W. MAYNARD." Above the two at the back is "A. MAYNARD." Above the three on the right is "L. MAYNARD." Some of

The crypt faces Route 27. The remains of twenty-two people are interred within.

Chiseled above the lintel are the year 1880 and the Greek letters alpha and omega entwined with a fleur-de-lis cross. Amory died ten years after having this built.

the vault doors have names and dates inscribed. In the center of the room is a large marble-topped table.

The crypt was competed in 1880, while Mary (1805–1886) and Amory (1804–1890) were still alive. They are both interred there, along with their third son, Harlan, who died in 1861 and was first buried in the cemetery, then later relocated to the crypt.

At one point in time, Amory's first son, Lorenzo, along with Lorenzo's wife and their four daughters, were also in the crypt, but in October 1904, Lorenzo's son arranged to have his six family members moved to a newly constructed mausoleum in Mount Auburn Cemetery in Cambridge, Massachusetts.

William, Amory's second son and his wife, Mary, are buried in Hope Cemetery in Worcester. They had moved to Worcester in 1888. Of their seven children, Mary S. Peters is the only Amory grandchild buried in Maynard. Also there are her husband, Warren Peters, their four daughters (Mary, Irene, Nettie, Bertha) and Mary's and Irene's husbands, Frank Sanderson and Leonard Henderson. Mary Sanderson (1874–1947) was the last Maynard descendant to live in Maynard.

William's son Amory, in some accounts referred to as Amory II, so as not to be confused with his grandfather, buried his first wife, Ida, and their infant daughter, Lola, in the crypt in 1881. But he and his second wife are buried elsewhere—site unknown.

The other bodies in residence are descendants of William's son Harlan. Even though Harlan and his wife, Florence, are not in the crypt, the tally includes six of their children and three of their grandchildren. The last interment on record occurred in 2006. There are descendants alive today, but it is not known whether anyone intends to add to the population.

3

NINETEENTH CENTURY

This one-hundred-year period witnessed the radical transformation of Assabet Village from a few dozen impoverished hill farmers and a gristmill to an urban center of three thousand people, with a train station, hotels and downtown streets lined with stores, restaurants and bars. The mill or the Maynard family owned most of the housing.

Massachusetts: First Colony to Legalize Slavery

Massachusetts was the first British colony to legalize slavery. The year 1641 saw the passing of the Massachusetts Body of Liberties. This set of ninety-eight edicts established rules of law governing how men, women, children and servants had essential rights. Rule 91 stated that there shall never be slavery, serfdom or captivity "unless it be lawful captives taken in just wars, and such strangers as willingly sell themselves or are sold to us."

And there it was: strangers sold to us could be owned as slaves. And, de facto, their children.

Prior to 1641, there had been a handful of slaves owned by colonists. The real impetus for this part of the Body of Liberties was war with Native Americans. The colonists did not want to free their captives from these wars—men, women and children—but could not decide what to do with them. The decision was reached to sell them into slavery in the Caribbean colonies. Returning ships started to bring back a few Negro slaves as cargo.

Slavery never took hold in the northern colonies as it did in the southern colonies, mostly because there were no labor-intensive cash crops—no tobacco, no indigo and no rice. (Cotton as a slave-worked crop developed only after the invention of the cotton gin in 1793.) Instead, northern slaves were primarily prestige property for the upper class, especially for educated men who did not intend to have themselves or their wives do much physical labor about the home and farm.

These ministers, lawyers, doctors, judges and military officers typically owned one to three slaves. Increase Mather, president of Harvard College, owned slaves, as did his minister son, Cotton Mather, author of *Rules for the Society of Negroes* and *The Negro Christianized*.

By the numbers: 550 adult slaves in Massachusetts, by 1708, had grown to 2,720 in the town-by-town slave census conducted in 1754. This was a bit more than 1 percent of the total population but was heavily skewed toward higher percentages in Boston and coastal cities. Boston was 10 percent Negro in 1754 (counting slave and free). In that same census year, Concord was recorded as having 15 adult slaves age sixteen or older, Sudbury 14, Acton 1 and Stow none. Maynard did not yet exist as a separate town.

The end of slavery in Massachusetts was hastened by the Revolutionary War. Many Loyalists fled to British-controlled territory, often abandoning their slaves. To disrupt the colonial efforts against them, the British army publicized that it would free slaves. The Continental army, under the command of slave owner George Washington, initially opposed enrolling any Negro men but soon changed this edict. Free Negroes were allowed to enroll, and slave owners received a cash compensation for any slave freed to then serve in the army for a set period of time.

Massachusetts was the first of the newly forming states to end slavery. With the war still raging on, Massachusetts passed a state constitution in 1780. Key wording: "All men are born free and equal, and have certain natural, essential, and unalienable rights; among which may be reckoned the right of enjoying and defending their lives and liberties; that of acquiring, possessing, and protecting property; in fine, that of seeking and obtaining their safety and happiness."

The state legislature may not have intended this to mean the end of slavery; draft versions proposed in 1777 and 1778 had been clear that slavery would continue. But the 1780 wording was what became law. Within a few years, court cases were brought on behalf of people who claimed they could no longer be owned.

A key decision in 1783 by the Supreme Judicial Court of Massachusetts came down against slave ownership. In 1788, the state passed a law prohibiting the buying, selling or transporting of Africans as slaves and made illegal the transport of any people from Massachusetts to sell as slaves elsewhere.

Were there slaves owned in what later became Maynard? Apparently not. Northern Sudbury and eastern Stow (the land that later became Maynard) was poor farmland, thinly settled and distant from the centers of those two towns, where the more prosperous slave-owning residents lived.

Thoreau Walked Through

Henry David Thoreau died in 1862, nine years before the founding of Maynard. This is not to say that he did not visit the area. Transcripts of his journals yield mention of the Assabet River, the gunpowder mill, the paper mill and the newly constructed dam built for the woolen mill.

On September 4, 1851, Thoreau set out with William Ellery Channing (whom he referred to as "W.E.C." or "C." in his journals) to walk from Concord to Boon Lake and back. The round-trip distance was a tad over twenty miles, some of it on roads or along the railroad and some through woods and fields. Outward bound, he notes that chemical odors from the gunpowder mill made them cough. Their walk continued westward past the paper mill, meaning that they were walking through what was then known as Assabet Village—now Maynard—possibly on Main Street, which had been constructed in 1848. At the time of his visit, the mills of Assabet Village were the business center of a population of about eight hundred people.

On the way back from Boon Lake, Thoreau and Channing walked alongside the railroad, on the south side of the Assabet River. Thoreau complained in his journal that there was no good place to bathe for three miles because Knight's new dam (the Ben Smith dam, constructed in 1846–47) had so raised the river. His description: "The fluviatile [meaning found near or in rivers] trees standing dead for fish hawk perches and the water stagnant for weeds to grow in." Thoreau also wrote that on the way back to Concord, they rested on the top of a hill looking down on a new brick icehouse—most likely N.J. Wyeth's brick icehouse, built in 1849, by the millpond.

As we well know, Thoreau was an avid walker long before people thought of this activity as a valid adult pastime. *Walking* is the title of a collection of his writings on the topic. His first public reading was at the Concord

During summer's dry times, barely any water trickles over the Ben Smith Dam. In his journal, Thoreau used fancy words to complain that this dam made the river stagnant and thus unfit for bathing.

Lyceum on April 23, 1851. Between 1851 and 1860, Thoreau read from the piece a total of ten times, more than any other of his lectures. *Walking* was published in the June 1862 issue of the *Atlantic Monthly*, shortly after his death from tuberculosis at age forty-four. The essay's length is slightly more than twelve thousand words. Various Internet sources have the complete essay available online—some with researchers' annotations. Thoreau gives his views on "wildness": "The West of which I speak is but another name for the Wild; and what I have been preparing to say is, that in Wildness is the preservation of the world." This is oft quoted as a fragment: "In Wildness [not "Wilderness"] is the preservation of the world." Thoreau felt that it was necessary for one's soul to be able to walk in wildness every day.

Thoreau was not a casual walker. He wrote:

> *It is true, we are but faint hearted crusaders, even the walkers, now-a-days,*
> *who undertake no persevering, never-ending enterprises. Our expeditions are*
> *but tours and come round again at evening to the old hearth side from which*

we set out. Half the walk is but retracing our steps. We should go forth on the shortest walk, perchance, in the spirit of undying adventure, never to return; prepared to send back our embalmed hearts only, as relics to our desolate kingdoms. If you are ready to leave father and mother, and brother and sister, and wife and child and friends, and never see them again; if you have paid your debts, and made your will, and settled all your affairs, and are a free man; then you are ready for a walk.

Thoreau's opinions were not humble opinions:

I think that I cannot preserve my health and spirits unless I spend four hours a day at least—and it is commonly more than that—sauntering through the woods and over the hills and fields absolutely free from all worldly engagements... When sometimes I am reminded that the mechanics and shop-keepers stay in their shops not only all the forenoon, but all the afternoon too, sitting with crossed legs, so many of them—as if the legs were made to sit upon, and not to stand or walk upon—I think that they deserve some credit for not having all committed suicide long ago.

Thoreau was aghast at the idea of exercise for its own sake:

But the walking of which I speak has nothing in it akin to taking exercise, as it is called, as the sick take medicine at stated hours—as the swinging of dumb-bells or chairs; but is itself the enterprise and adventure of the day. If you would get exercise go in search of the springs of life. Think of a man's swinging dumb-bells for his health, when those springs are bubbling up in far off pastures unsought by him.

Thoreau cherished the meditative rewards of wilderness walking:

I am alarmed when it happens that I have walked a mile into the woods bodily, without getting there in spirit. In my afternoon walk I would fain forget all my morning occupations, and my obligations to society. But it sometimes happens that I cannot easily shake off the village. The thought of some work will run in my head, and I am not where my body is; I am out of my senses. In my walks I would fain return to my senses. What business have I in the woods, if I am thinking of something out of the woods?

The Paper Mill

"Money for old rope" is a saying more commonly heard in England than in the United States. The phrase means money you get for doing something that is very easy or from selling something that is normally considered nearly worthless. Origins of this saying are disputed, but one explanation pertains to the manufacture of paper.

Once upon a time, rope was made from fibers from hemp plants. When it wore out, it was unraveled to use for other purposes, such as ships' caulking. This stuff, called oakum, was hammered into the seams between planks of a ship and then tarred for waterproofing purposes; thus, monetary value for old rope. Alternatively, the saying is thought to have come from using old rope for papermaking. Prior to the mid-1800s, the raw material for paper was linen rags, cotton rags or unraveled rope, each finely shredded and pounded to create the very short fibers needed for paper. Using wood fiber for paper came later.

William May built a paper mill on the Sudbury side of the Assabet River in 1820. This means the first dam on the Assabet River was not for Maynard's wool mill in 1847 but rather the paper mill's dam, decades earlier. An August 1914 newspaper account of the demise of the last vestige of the paper mill—its chimney—mentioned that the mill had used rags and rope as raw materials.

William May was not successful in his endeavor. He sold to John Sawyer, who in turn sold the mill to William Parker. In February 1831, Parker and his partners, Samuel Townsend and Peter C. Jones, incorporated the operation as the Fourdrinier Paper Company.

Why that name? At the beginnings of the nineteenth century, the Fourdrinier brothers, in England, were perfecting and patenting a papermaking process that made a continuous roll of paper as opposed to the old method of making paper by hand, one sheet at a time. Historical records state that the first Fourdrinier machine imported to the United States arrived in 1827. Parker's choice of name for his company promoted the message that he was using the most advanced papermaking technology available at the time.

Parker's mill ran for sixty years, originally powered by a water wheel but later by coal-fired steam engine (hence the chimney that needed to be razed). An etching of an aerial view of the town of Maynard, dated 1879, showed a sizable mill and a smoke-emitting chimney.

In 1840, a bridge was constructed just downstream from the mill—the Paper Mill Bridge. Looking upriver from the bridge gave a fine view of

The paper mill was situated on the south bank of the Assabet River, southwest of the Waltham Street Bridge. *Courtesy of Maynard Historical Society.*

the Paper Mill Dam. The dam was known locally as The Falls for the way water cascaded down the rough stone face. Dam and bridge were both destroyed in the flood of 1927. The bridge was rebuilt in 1928 and that one replaced in 2013.

The paper mill was purchased by Maynard & Hemenway, a company co-owned by William Maynard (Amory Maynard's son), in 1882. The new owners did not operate the factory. Rather, it was used as a warehouse for the Assabet Woolen Company. There was a fire of suspicious origin on the morning of May 12, 1894. The fire department succeeded in quenching the flames.

Two days later, the mill was on fire again (and again, arson was suspected), but this time it burned to the ground. All that remained was the chimney, which stood "as a gloomy monument to the past" for twenty years more.

Back to rope and money. A different origin story has ties to the days of public executions. The hangman's perquisite was to keep the rope used to hang his "customer." Pieces of such a rope were highly valued as bringing good luck to gamblers, so the hangman would sell pieces and made "money for old rope."

Water Power

Deep in the bowels of Clock Tower Place, there is a space where an antiquated monster once sat—the turbine that converted water power to electrical power. This machine was the last of several generations of hydropower-generating engineering in the mill.

Hydropower is all about high school algebra: vertical drop in feet times flow in gallons per minute divided by ten thousand equals kilowatts, and kW x 1.34 equals horsepower. For the metric-minded, vertical drop in meters times flow in liters per second times 9.81 divided by one thousand also equals kilowatts. By this math, ten gallons of water dropping one hundred feet yields the same power as one hundred gallons of water falling ten feet.

Actual power yield is always less than theoretical due to friction and other inefficiencies. An "undershot" water wheel describes a design with water running under the wheel, pushing the bottom blades forward. For wooden wheels of this design, capture of the water's energy was on the order of 20 to 30 percent.

Wherever greater vertical drop allowed, water was led over the top of the wheel to pull blades downward by force of gravity. This style, referred to as "overshot," traditionally captured 50 to 70 percent of available energy. By the 1830s, wheels would have had wooden blades, rims and spokes attached to iron hubs and axles. Late in the 1800s, the Fitz Waterwheel Company was selling all-steel water wheels, with the advantages of nearly 90 percent efficiency plus resistance to icing in winter.

Back to Maynard, or what at the time was known as Assabet Village. Construction of the Ben Smith Dam, the millpond and the canal between the two in 1847 resulted in a large, year-round water reserve at an altitude above sea level of 175 feet. Outflow from the waterworks would have reentered Assabet River below the mill at an altitude of 160 feet. Flow rate through the system is not known, nor is there any record of the design, but a good guess is two overshot wheels each with a 15-foot drop and a combined flow of up to forty-five thousand gallons per minute.

That flow is equivalent to one hundred cubic feet of water per second (cfs). For comparison, the Assabet River has a year-round average of two hundred cfs, but summer months average under one hundred cfs. Keep in mind that water power production was never around the clock. Flow through the mill was stopped at the end of the workday to back up as much water as possible in the millpond for the next day.

Power production was approximately fifty horsepower. As Maynard's mill operations grew, water power was supplemented by coal-fueled steam power, hence all the historic images with smokestacks. The book *Assabet Mills* states that by 1879, nearly 40 percent of power was from steam engines.

At some point, the water wheel complex was replaced by a turbine. Turbines are much more compact than wheels. Water drops down through a progressively narrowing pipe. This water, now under high pressure, jets into the turbine chamber at high speed, spins the turbine blades and exits out the bottom. Turbine efficiencies rival the best wheels.

According to an article in the March 14, 1902 issue of the *Maynard News*, the switch to electric power included the installation of two vertical compound engines directly connected to electric generators. The engines would have been steam engines powered by either coal or fuel oil. The power of the two engines was 2,500 and 800 horsepower. From this time forward, hydropower was clearly a minor portion of total energy production at the mill complex. At the time, employment at the mill was two thousand men, women and children.

Records show a hydroturbine used to generate electricity from 1902 to 1968. Digital Equipment Corporation refurbished the power plant in 1983 and ran it until 1992. The Clock Tower Place 2002 petition to surrender electricity-generating rights described the last operative turbine as having a pass-through of 128 cfs and production of 125 kilowatts of energy. Today, the turbine is long gone, the smokestack is merely a support for cellphone antennae and all of the kilowatt hours used to power Clock Tower Place by day and light up the windows by night are wired in from elsewhere. The future may see solar panels on the roof.

The Clock Tower Clock

According to Arnold (Skip) Wilson, "Until I retired in 2012, I was responsible for winding the clock in the Clock Tower for almost twenty-five years. This job needs to be done once a week, so I figure since 1892, it's been wound more than six thousand times." Responsibility passed from Wilson to Leon Tyler.

Lorenzo Maynard arranged for construction of the tower and clock as a memorial to his father, Amory Maynard, cofounder of the mill, who had passed away in 1890. The tower was built from the ground up, with the lower half between two existing buildings. The red-and-white-painted top third is made of wood. The tower's official dedication was on October 23, 1892. The clock's four faces have always been illuminated by electric lights. While the clock mechanism is original, Digital Equipment Corporation completely renovated the tower in 1980.

The clock is hand-wound, making it one of the few public clocks in New England to do without electric power. Every Monday, an employee of Clock Tower Place climbs the wooden steps to turn cranks that raise weights to provide power to the clock and the bell striker. When fully wound, the weights provide power for eight days.

To visualize the clock, think of it as the grandfather of all grandfather clocks. The room is twelve by twelve feet. Each clock face is nine feet across. The clock mechanism is mounted in a frame about the size of a dining room table, securely bolted to the floor. The pendulum is nine feet long. It extends through a slot in the floor to the room below. Over each week, the weights—suspended by steel cables—slowly descend from the tower to just above the first floor.

Operating directions on the original piece of paper from 1892 are posted inside the tower. Wilson said that the clock mechanism is so accurate that it is

Gears behind one of the four clock faces turn the minute and hour hands.

A vertical shaft rotates the crown gear, which drives the four sets of face gears.

off by, at most, one minute a month. Routine maintenance does not require much beyond the occasional oiling which is good because the company that made the clock, E. Howard & Co., from Boston, stopped making tower clocks in 1964.

Lighting the face of the clock is now managed with fluorescent light bulbs, eight per face. On the special occasions when color is added to the lighting, the method is simple: colored plastic tubes are slipped over the lights. The faces are lit orange around Thanksgiving, to coincide with the Maynard High School homecoming football game. Red and green lead up to winter holidays. Blue appeared for the first time in April 2012 to acknowledge World Autism Awareness Day. The tower itself was originally painted in red and white, redone in gray and white from 1942 to 1998 and then reverted to the original colors it sports today.

For many years, Maynard's fifth-grade classes made a field trip to the clock tower. Students would ascend the ever-steepening wooden stairs to the cramped room that houses the clock's mechanism to see the pendulum, escarpment, crown gear that drives the four face gears and the triggering

Clock face showing the iconic 12:10 time, which was incorporated into a revision of the town seal in 1975. Note 4:00 is shown as IIII rather than IV.

mechanism for the bell striker. Sadly, the trips are no more—the school's decision—so students no longer gain firsthand memory of something that helps makes their town different from most.

The Town Tried to Change Its Name

Maynard almost changed its name thirty-one years after it was founded. Impetus for the name change seemed to be three-fold: American Woolen Company, the new owner of the mill complex, wanted the name change; people were still angry that Amory Maynard, mill founder, had not left a significant gift to the town when he died in 1890; and his son, Lorenzo Maynard, was accused of mismanaging operations of the mill to the point that it fell into bankruptcy at the end of 1898, costing many millworkers their jobs plus part of their savings, which they had entrusted to the Assabet Manufacturing Company, as there was no bank in town.

Lorenzo Maynard built this mansion on the hill south of the mill, a short distance away from his father's even larger mansion. An 1889 map shows a reflecting pond in front and a greenhouse on one side. The building is currently apartments but is still graced with some of the original stained-glass windows.

A petition filed with the state's Committee on Towns on February 4, 1902, by James B. Lord and a few other townspeople plus the American Woolen Co. became House Bill No. 903, "An Act to Change the Name of the Town of Maynard." The petition's intent was to change the name of the town to Assabet. The bill called for a majority vote by the legal voters of the town at a special town meeting, with the meeting to be held within ninety days of the passage of the bill. Hearings on the petition were held on March 11, 18, 25 (that one in Maynard) and 28. The topic was well covered by local newspapers.

It is not entirely clear why the American Woolen Company waited for two years after acquiring the bankrupt mill, although one newspaper account mentioned unhappiness with Lorenzo Maynard after he refused to sell land to the American Woolen Company. At about this time, Amory Maynard II (Amory's grandson, Lorenzo's nephew) was abruptly fired from his management position at the mill.

A February 11, 1902 letter from American Woolen Company to local newspapers gave as reasons for the change that it would take less time to stencil the revised corporate information on packing cases; that the new business was solely men's wear, whereas the previous product line had been for the dress goods business; and "other sundry reasons." The petition took many people by surprise. Opposition formed, especially from the longer-term inhabitants.

The March 28, 1902 issue of the *Maynard News* led off with these headlines:

MAYNARD OR WHAT?
Hearing on Change of Name
Arguments For and Against
American Woolen Co. Desires Change

The following paragraphs are excerpts from the article:

The legislative hearing on the petition for a change in the name of the town was continued on Tuesday. The hearing began at the State house, Boston, but after a two hours' session the hearing was continued for one week, the Commonwealth of Massachusetts Committee on Towns deciding to pay a visit to Maynard.

Mr. Murray, representing the petitioners for name change, called Julian Lowe, who stated that he had resided in Maynard about 29 years and had been in the wholesale and retail liquor business about 21 years. He signed the petition for a change of name, and in talking with others has found a decided sentiment existing in favor of the change. He had lost money by the failure of the Assabet Manufacturing Co., and at that time had heard considerable discussion relating to a change of name.

Ashael H. Haynes next appeared for the petitioners. He stated that he had been in the clothing business in Maynard 25 years. He favored the change and believed that the sentiment on town was also that way. Ralph Whitehead believed the sentiment in favor of the change was 3 to 1.

Mr. Murray then called upon James F. Sweeney, who as a life-long resident of Maynard, someone who had known Amory Maynard and knew him as an honest, businesslike man, was nevertheless strongly in favor of the change. Mr. Sweeney spoke of the influence exerted over the voters of the town when the Assabet mills were controlled by the Maynards, intimating that they dared not vote against the mill owners for fear the means of livelihood would be lost.

Mr. Sweeney charged the Maynards with being opposed to the installation of the public water system and the building of the present Nason street schoolhouse. He further stated that when the town was incorporated in 1871, the Maynard family and the Assabet Company owned nearly all the tenements in town. There were no sidewalks, street lights, and but poor educational advantages. He spoke of the lack of a Town Hall, and said that for many years the town had been obliged to pay a high rent for use of Riverside Hall, a building owned by the Maynard family.

He stated that for ten years before its downfall, the Assabet mills had been tottering, and that a few months previous to the failure Lorenzo Maynard, realizing that the end was drawing nigh, signed over property to the amount of $250,000 to protect himself when the crash came. Mr. Sweeney closed with an appeal to the Committee to allow the citizens the privilege of exercising their right to vote on the matter.

Thomas Hillis, in opening for the remonstrants, told of the founding of the original mill, and gave a brief history of Amory Maynard, its founder. He contrasted the size of the place when Amory Maynard first arrived in Assabet valley with the size of the town when Mr. Maynard retired in 1884.

"When Mr. Maynard first came here," said Mr. Hillis, "there were only 12 houses in the place; when he retired from business 1,200 hands were employed at the mills, and the mills had a surplus of $1,000,000 and paid six percent on its capital stock. When the town was incorporated it was given the name of Maynard by the voters, but the honor was not sought by Amory Maynard, and in yielding to the wishes of the townspeople he had made no promises of bequests or memorials in return for the use of his name."

Mr. Hillis added, "Because Lorenzo Maynard had failed was no reason why the name should be changed, and that he would show that prior to 1898 no one had ever thought of changing the name of the town."

Mr. M.H. Garfield, of the gunpowder mills, and Mr. John W. Ogden, superintendent of the trolley, spoke against the petition, as did Mr. Frank H. Harriman of Harriman Bros. Laundry. Mr. Harriman stated that his father had never heard Amory Maynard promising to give anything to the town, and further, that he did not believe in letting the people vote on the question.

Other people well known in Maynard spoke against the petition, among them William B. Case, owner of the dry goods store, the Reverend Edwin Smith, retired pastor of the Congregational Church, Abel G. Haynes, John Whitney and Artemas Whitney. In accord was Sidney B. Shattuck, who said that Maynard was good enough for him. He was decidedly against going back to the name "Assabet," as it was an Indian name and he had no use for Indians.

It should be noted that Sweeney's complaints about lack of schools, sidewalks, streetlights and town buildings prior to the incorporation of the town in 1871 were somewhat disingenuously directed toward Amory Maynard. Prior to that year, the land and peoples about the mill were either citizens of Stow (if north of the river) or Sudbury (if south). The main reason the locals petitioned to succeed from those parent towns was that they were being taxed but not getting the services they desired.

Furthermore, the newspaper accounts failed to mention that Amory Maynard had donated land for the construction of the Union Congregational Church and, according to the church pastor, was responsible for many other charitable acts. Nor did the paper mention that Lorenzo Maynard had personally paid for construction of the church annex and the Clock Tower.

There was a reservoir of ill will toward Lorenzo Maynard amongst the townspeople because of mismanagement of the Assabet Manufacturing Company, leading up to the declaration of bankruptcy at the end of 1898. A large part of the problem was that employees and ex-employees had approximately $132,000 held by AMC as a de facto savings bank. After the mill failed, only $70,000 was recovered by the people who had savings on deposit.

Highly relevant to why the mill failed, but not mentioned in any of the local historical accounts, was the fact that the U.S. government's Wilson-Gorman Tariff Act of 1894 had ended the protectionist tariffs on imported wool and other goods. This, plus the recession that started in 1893, put financial pressure on woolen mills throughout New England, not just in Maynard. Dozens failed. The federal government restored a protective tariff on importation of both raw wool and finished wool fabric in 1897, as part of the Dingley Tariff Act, but it was too late to save the Assabet Manufacturing Company.

Excerpts from the April 4, 1902 issue of the *Maynard News* further reported on the proposed name change:

The final hearing on the petition took place at the State House, Boston, last Friday morning [March 28], when closing arguments were heard. As in the previous sessions, Michael J. Murray of Boston appeared for the petitioners and Thomas Hillis of Maynard for the remonstrants.

After the American Woolen Company took over in 1900, it expanded the mill complex, adding building after building, until this was the largest woolen mill in New England.

Mr. Hillis again dwelt solely on the fact that the town was named for Amory Maynard and impressed upon the members of the committee that any happenings at the Assabet mills since the retirement of Amory Maynard should not be considered at all.

Mr. Murray presented figures relating to the amount of money lost by the residents of the town at the time of the downfall of the old company under Lorenzo Maynard, and argued in favor of the citizens of the town being given a chance to vote on the question of a change of name.

Both petitioners and remonstrants have many adherents. Among the former are many residents of the town who were heavy losers by the failure of the Assabet Manufacturing Company, and who consider this to be a sufficient reason for a change. Arrayed against these on the remonstrant side are those who contend that this has no connection with the issue, but is simply an exhibition of spite, directed against one who had no hand in the naming of the town. On either side of the debate, many citizens believe the matter should be settled by a vote.

The American Woolen Company is on the side of the petitioners, giving as its reason that a change of name would greatly facilitate its business. Still others are of the opinion that the failure of Amory Maynard to provide for, or erect, some substantial memorial building or make some gift to the town is sufficient reason for a change.

The remonstrants reply to this by saying that Amory Maynard never promised to give anything to the town, and did not ask to have the place named for him, but instead, discouraged the idea.

There is still another element, which, imbued with socialistic principles, is against anything and everything which is supposed to be in favor of the American Woolen Company.

Thus the incident closes until the legislature announces its decision on the question of granting the citizens the privilege of voting on the matter. If such a privilege is granted, the vote will probably not be taken before the November election.

The end of the second 1902 newspaper article returned the decision to the hands of the Commonwealth of Massachusetts Committee on Towns, either by its authoritative power or after a vote by the residents of Maynard. According to the book *History of Maynard, Massachusetts, 1871–1971*, the Committee on Towns voted on May 2, 1902, by a five-to-four vote to allow the bill to proceed, but on May 8, the full state legislature killed the bill by a vote of seventy-nine to sixty-nine to not allow a third reading of the bill. There was to be no local vote. Maynard remained Maynard.

Firefighting Through the Years

Boston's history mentions "Great Fires" of 1653, 1711, 1760 and 1872. Locally, construction of mills and farmhouses began near the Assabet River in the late 1600s. Expansion of Maynard's mills plus the arrival of the railroad in 1850 made the community grow. Surely, buildings caught fire in those days, yet while the Town of Maynard appointed three fire wardens at its very first town meeting in 1871, it did not get around to organizing a fire department until 1890, twenty years later. Why the delay?

One factor for Maynard's municipal involvement in firefighting not being a high priority was, basically, that there was not much a fire department could do. Well into the 1800s, "getting the wet stuff on the red stuff" meant men running to the fire with buckets and forming a bucket line from the nearest well. Water would either be thrown directly at the fire or poured into a tank on a fire wagon, wherein hand-powered pumps provided water pressure. Later innovations included leather hoses and hook and ladder wagons.

The historical archives from Sudbury, which Maynard was part of until 1871, are informative. As early as 1666, selectmen's meetings ordered every household to have a ladder of sufficient length to reach the roof of the house for extinguishing of fires. The town's fire wardens could impose fines of ten shillings for failure to comply. Yet Sudbury did not have a salaried fire department until 1931.

Firefighting in cities was more advanced. American cities began to install reservoirs and water mains toward the end of the 1700s. Equipment purchases and payments became municipal responsibilities supported by local taxes. Water pipes were sometimes hollowed-out logs. When water was needed for a fire, firefighters would dig down to the pipe and then chop a hole in the log to access water. Afterward, someone would rough-cut a piece of wood and hammer it into the hole as a plug. When hydrants were introduced, they were called fireplugs.

Cast-iron fire hydrants, akin to what we have now, started appearing in the early 1800s. Steam-powered pumps on horse-drawn wagons did

Firefighters pose at the corner of Nason and Main Streets, in front of the smoldering remains of the Naylor Block fire. *Courtesy of Maynard Historical Society.*

not put in an appearance until after the Civil War, and then only in larger cities.

In Maynard, a town reservoir was constructed in 1888 on Summer Hill. A water delivery system, including fifty-seven fire hydrants, was completed in 1889. Maynard's first fire station was constructed at 36 Nason Street in 1890. The site is currently occupied by the Paper Store. The initial major pieces of equipment were a hose wagon and a ladder wagon. Men committed to showing up as quickly as possible when the alarm sounded. The first full-time employee was hired in 1903. The first gas-powered fire truck was purchased in 1914.

The original firehouse served until 1955, when the current building on Summer Street was completed, with five thousand square feet dedicated to fire station operations. Construction costs of $144,115 were less than what one ladder truck costs now. Town documents described the fire department as having two firemen on duty at all times, with the off-duty men on call, two pieces of equipment (fire truck and ladder truck) and servicing 150 to 200 incidents per year. By 2005, on-duty staff had increased to five, vehicles to seven and incidents to 600 to 800 per year, out of the same space. Obviously, not all incidents are fires or else the entire town would have burned several times over!

Big Fires

There were many fires that changed Maynard, or at least the architecture of Maynard. Compilation of various records for the gunpowder mills found twenty-four explosions and twenty-nine fatalities. The paper mill had been closed for years before it was destroyed by a fire reputed to be arson. A wool mill fire in 1920 meant the end of buildings dating back to 1846.

Not listed in the table on page 55, Booth's Bowling Alley burned in July 6, 1906. Suspicions at the time were that a pet monkey that had the run of the place at night and knew how to strike matches was responsible for the fire (the monkey suffered burns but survived).

After the trolley's building and rolling stock went up in flames, the brick building was rebuilt and replacement cars purchased, but the line was already in financial decline. Trolley service ended with a last run on January 16, 1923. Today, the building houses offices. Upstream of the dam, the Bent Ice House burned in February 1919. A replacement was built on the same foundation. That one burned in November 1950.

Table III
DATES AND DESCRIPTIONS OF SOME OF THE LARGER FIRES

DATE	WHAT BURNED	BUILT AFTER	THERE NOW
1835–1940	gunpowder mill	gunpowder mill	Stop & Shop plaza, car dealers
5/14/1894	paper mill	?????	Tedeschi's, Dunkin' Donuts
11/26/12	music hall	Tutto's Bowling Alley	recently torn store/apartment buildings
9/20/16	Nason Street School	Roosevelt School	Maynard Public Library
2/11/17	Naylor Block	one-story storefronts	Gallery Seven, Serendipity, Little Pusan
1/25/18	trolley building	rebuilt	Millpond Square office building
2/1/19	Bent Ice House	another icehouse	that one burned in 1950
8/17/20	wool mill	more mill buildings	Clock Tower buildings
1/29/21	Maynard Hotel	Memorial Park	Memorial Park
7/14/34	Riverside Block	same building, fixed	Gruber Bros. Furniture
1/30/36	Riverside Co-op	brick building	Knights of Columbus
12/17/52	Woodrow Wilson School	town hall and library	town hall and police station
3/13/55	Fraternal Order of Eagles	two-story building	Masciarelli Jewelry
7/29/65	Amory Maynard's house	apartment building	apartment building

Amory Maynard's mansion is the only private dwelling listed in the table above (although many others went up in flames). It was built on the hill south of the mill in 1873 and succumbed to an early morning fire on July 29, 1965. The Maynard family was long gone from town. His son's former house still stands at 5–7 Dartmouth Street. It is divided into apartments but provides semblance to Amory's larger mansion.

In the modern era, the two-story building on Main Street that housed Salsalito's Restaurant and T.C. Lando's Sub & Pizzeria was consumed by flames in 1998, NAPA Auto Parts ditto in 2001; Gruber Bros. Furniture suffered a smoky fire a handful of years ago.

To paraphrase Robert Frost, someone there is that doesn't love a school (often a student). This is not to hint that school fires do not happen by

The Maynard Hotel fire started in the kitchen. *Courtesy of Maynard Historical Society.*

accident. But history records five school fires (the two in the table, plus Nason Street School in 1879, Emerson-Fowler School in 1977 and Maynard High School in 1992) but no record of any church fires.

4

TWENTIETH CENTURY

This century saw the decline of one major influence (the woolen mill under American Woolen Company) and the rise (and then fall) of a second (Digital Equipment Corporation). The population more than tripled to 10,400. The century ended with great promise, as the mill complex was again filling with businesses.

Remembering War Veterans

At the corner of Summer and Concord Streets, a bit west of ArtSpace, there is a plaque on a metal pole reading, "Anthony Dzerkacz Square." There are other plaques scattered about Maynard honoring George Daley, Frank J. DeMars, Frank G. King, Edward Miller, John R. Murray, Ralph I. Panton and Myles J. Tierney. A visit to Memorial Park reveals these men as having died in World War I. The American Legion Post on Summer Street is named for DeMars, as he was the first from Maynard to give his life in the service of his country during that war.

Maynard does not memorialize its Revolutionary and Civil War veterans by name, for the simple reason of the town not existing prior to 1871 except as part of Stow and Sudbury. Stow's minutemen marched through what later became Maynard on the morning of April 19, 1775, on their way to Concord. The march is reenacted every Patriots' Day.

Dedication of the War Memorial, November 15, 1925. The memorial was constructed on the site of the Maynard Hotel, which burned in 1921. The land occupied by buildings in the near background is now a parking lot.

Hometown Soldiers: Civil War Veterans of Assabet Village and Maynard Massachusetts, by Peggy Jo Brown, avid amateur historian, documents the lives and final resting places of those Maynard residents who served in the Civil War. According to Brown, the first person officially buried in St. Bridget's Cemetery was James Heffernan, a Civil War veteran.

Maynard's Memorial Park monuments list the men and women who served in the two world wars, Korea and Vietnam. A few names can be linked to older conflicts. Joel F. Parmenter and Daniel L. Parmenter served in World War I. Their great-great-great-grandfather Deliverance Parmenter Jr. served during the Revolutionary War, as did his brother, Jason. Less than ten years after that war ended, Jason was active in Shay's Rebellion, a Massachusetts taxpayers' revolt against state property taxes established to pay off the war debt. Jason was sentenced to be executed for killing a federal agent. He was pardoned at the last moment by Governor John Hancock.

During the early years of World War I, President Woodrow Wilson approved the concept of a service flag with a blue star to be displayed at homes of families with members serving in the armed forces—one star for each person serving. If a person died in service, the blue star was replaced by a gold star. The stars on the plaques memorializing Maynard's World War I dead are emblematic of their families' gold stars.

Karen Hamilton of Maynard shared a transcript of one sailor's experiences in the Great War. The American Woolen Company gave each employee who enrolled in the armed forces a diary book to record his war experiences. Carl Alexander (Allie) Petersen, Hamilton's godfather, enlisted in the U.S. Navy Reserve Force in December 1917 and was assigned to active duty a few weeks later. Navy records misspelled his surname as Peterson. He was twenty-two years old.

Petersen logged 568 days of active service, including five round-trip crossings of the Atlantic Ocean, before being relieved from active duty in 1919. Petersen's first crossing was on the USS *South Dakota*, an armored cruiser providing convoy escort service. He was subsequently transferred to a 340-foot-long tanker the *Wieldrecht*. This Dutch ship had been at harbor at New York City. The U.S. Navy seized it by right of angary. After the war, the navy returned it to the Dutch owners.

Over time, Petersen was promoted to third-class petty officer. On the USS *Wieldrecht*, his assignment was gun pointer for the five-inch-diameter gun mounted forward. He also at times served as helmsman.

Petersen made hundreds of diary entries. On July 4, 1918, he complained that he did not rate liberty while in port and instead spent more than twelve hours rowing other sailors to and from the ship. His entry for July 13, 1918, reads, "Brooks died this morning. We gave him Military Funeral. Sewed him in canvas with 5 inch shell and gently let him overboard. Mess Cook played Taps. Skipper prayed from the Bible. During the ceremony five Transports passed us. We had a time finding a Bible."

The *Wieldrecht* transported airplane fuel, so the risk of fire and explosion was high. German submarines were sighted twice. One was sunk by an escorting destroyer's depth charges. Because of the *Wieldrecht*'s slow speed—about eleven miles per hour—it often was unable to keep up with a convoy and so finished some crossings alone. Atlantic storms were always a risk. Petersen's entry from December 18, 1918, was: "Bad storm. We may go down." And the next day: "Still bad. Miracle we are still afloat." But in the end, he lived to leave the navy, to marry, to be commander of Maynard's American Legion Post and to die in 1965 at the age of seventy.

Come Memorial Day, flags placed by American Legion volunteers mark the graves of those who served. Modest parades pass through downtown

Children holding American flags at the 2013 Veterans Day ceremony. The parking deck behind them was torn down in 2014 because the concrete was deteriorating.

to commemorate that date and also for Veterans Day, in the fall. Everyone should take time off from holiday sales events and backyard barbecues to acknowledge what we are remembering.

ON A PERSONAL NOTE, my father was a private in the U.S. Army, 106th Infantry Division, awarded, among other medals, a Bronze Star and a Purple Heart. He was captured at the Battle of the Bulge and later imprisoned at the notorious Berga an der Estler Prison. U.S. POWs were sent to Berga if their army IDs identified them as Jewish or if they "looked Jewish." Of the 350 at Berga, from February 1945 until they were liberated two months later, nearly half died from a combination of starvation, cold and disease or by execution for trying to escape. After the war, my father completed a doctorate in clinical psychology from New York University and worked in that field until he retired at age eighty. He passed away in 2011, at age ninety-one. He is remembered by friends and family, including Stella Mark, his wife of sixty-eight years, children and grandchildren.

Before National Prohibition:
Locally Voting Wet or Dry

In 1911, at the March town meeting, Maynard voted to stay "wet" on the issue of local option prohibition, with the vote tally at 467 to 340. Maynard remained wet through 1914 but voted itself "dry" by a tally of 521 to 519 in 1915. "Wet" meant that the town would continue to license saloons and liquor stores to operate legally. A "dry" vote would suspend the sale of alcohol.

Hudson was going through similar gyrations. Ten years earlier, the votes were consistently pro-licensing. Later, Hudson voted itself dry in 1910, wet in 1911 and then back to dry in 1912. Just before national Prohibition went into effect in 1920, the majority of towns in Massachusetts were already dry, while Maynard was still wet.

The March 9, 1900 edition of the *Maynard News* ran a large front-page advertisement that read, "Why Maynard Should Have Licenses." Among the arguments: "License means more business, more money [saloons paid taxes], less drunkenness, a better standing in the commercial world and the life of a progressive town, while no-license means stagnation, dives, kitchen barrooms, vile liquors, more policemen, higher taxes and no satisfaction."

Wet did not always win. The year 1903 saw a dry vote in Maynard by 379 to 301, after nine straight years of pro-wet voting. The 1904 vote stayed dry, perhaps influenced by an impassioned pre-vote letter in the newspaper reading, in part:

> *Maynard as it is today, or Maynard as it was a year ago; Maynard with the streets clear of the hideous sight of a reeling drunkard, or Maynard with the police records showing as many as seven and eight arrests in one day, as was often the case not more than a year ago; Maynard with its midnight street brawls and saloon carousals resulting in the sight of human gore spilled on the streets and in the saloon...or Maynard as it stands today, a clean and respectable town, with these disreputable and horrible conditions wiped out.*

Regardless, the 1905 vote reverted to wet by 451 to 361. The newspaper mentioned that the town intended to grant five licenses to sell liquor.

Anti-alcohol sentiments had had a long, long history in America. Sermons and speechifying against the evils of alcohol waxed during the early 1800s, waned with the Civil War and then built strength again with the Industrial Revolution's growth of cities, as factory jobs put more cash and opportunity to drink into the hands of working men than farm labor ever had.

Saloons were a place to stop for a shot or two (or three, or four) before heading home. Married men might find their wives and children at the factory gate at the end of payday, hoping to shame their husbands into handing over money for rent, groceries and such before they made it to the saloons and pool halls.

Successfully prohibiting alcohol was a bottom-up strategy. Shortly before 1900, the Anti-Saloon League developed a plan of campaigning for towns, counties and states to vote themselves dry. The ASL succeeded where the Woman's Christian Temperance Union and other temperance organizations had failed by making its cause a single-cause issue in close elections. Democrats, Republicans, whatever political party—no ASL support unless the candidate supported the cause.

One major barrier fell when the federal government approved collection of a federal income tax. Prior to this new revenue stream, as much as one-third of the federal budget had come from taxes on alcohol sales. Another fallen barrier hinged on the nature of World War I. German Americans, funded by money from German immigrant–owned beer companies such as Miller, Anheuser-Busch and Schlitz, lobbied politicians to oppose Prohibition. Because of the war, anti-German sentiments allowed these politicians to distance themselves from the idea of exempting beer from the proposed ban.

Collectively, all this anti-alcohol activity led to Prohibition going into effect nationwide. The federal law was fatally flawed from the beginning. Federal enforcement was underfunded. Prohibition proved to be wildly unpopular, and was repealed in 1933. Localities could still vote themselves dry. Lincoln, Weston and Harvard were still dry as late as 2007 but are now all wet.

Leapin' Lena: The American Legion's Parade Car

Residents with long memories can tell tales of a tricked-out car that participated in Maynard parades from 1927 into the early 1960s. Leapin' Lena was built through the efforts of Frank Parks, Ray Carruth, Joseph Dineen, Eddie Johnson and other men associated with the local American Legion Post #235. Frank and Ray had been inspired by a stunt car they saw at a performance of the Barnum & Bailey Circus. The American Legion crew started with an open-topped Ford Model T. The wheelbase was shortened, the car body was shifted back, concrete was used to add weight to the rear and steel skid plates were bolted to the underside of the back end.

Leapin' Lena in repose, eighteen years after her last public appearance. *Courtesy of Maynard Historical Society.*

With two people seated in front and three in back, Lena was so carefully balanced over the rear axle that a bit of acceleration, combined with the occupants leaning back, would pop her nose up to a twenty-degree angle. She could be driven a short distance in this nose-up position and then be slammed back down to the pavement with a touch of brakes—hard on the occupants!

A large, striped beach umbrella was mounted over the rear seat to provide shade. At the back, a small cannon loaded with ten-gauge shotgun blanks emitted smoky explosions.

Over years of hard-pounding parade performances, many of Lena's original parts failed, and Model A parts were spliced in as replacements. The frame became a crisscross of welds over welds. Motors burned out, and replacements were made. Lena spent the World War II years in hidden outside storage to avoid being swept up in the war's metal drives.

In addition to appearing in Maynard's parades, Leapin' Lena was transported to American Legion national conventions, including repeat appearances in New York City in 1930, 1937 and 1947. According to Legion lore, California congressman Richard M. Nixon, World War II veteran and

American Legion member, rode in the front seat in the 1947 parade. Nixon's comment, once the car bucked up, was along the lines of: "What are you trying to do, kill me?"

Maynard's Lena had the words "Original Leapin' Lena" painted across the back. As it turns out, quite a few American Legion and Shriner parades featured modified Model T cars—almost always named Leapin' Lena or Leaping Lena. But Maynard claimed to be the first. One car still puts in appearances at New Hampshire parades, another in Indiana.

There was also a wind-up-powered toy car, around 1925, named both Dizzie Lizzie (on the back) and Leaping Lena (on top). As it moved forward, it repeatedly reared up, leveled out and rocked from side to side. The date of the toy raises the question—which came first, the name or the various tricked-out cars? The answer is the former. The reason? Model T cars had only two gears, low and high. When the leftmost foot pedal was fully depressed, the car was in low gear. Easing off on the pedal took the car through neutral and then into high gear. Most drivers could not manage this without the car jolting roughly forward. As a result, Leaping Lena was a common nickname; other monikers were Bouncing Betty and Spirit of Saint Vitus (for the bone-jolting ride).

Leapin' Lena retired around 1962. A prolonged restoration led to a last attempt at a public appearance for the 1971 Maynard Centennial Parade. She performed well in a Crowe Park rehearsal but broke down partway through the parade. Many years later, the car, or what was left of her after years of haphazard storage, was close to being sold to the Maynard Antique Auto Club for the sum of one dollar, with intent to restore, but at the final hour, MAAC changed its mind and the car fell into the hands of Donny Crowther, who had the same intent.

Where things stand in 2014: Lena is in pieces but with the potential for a phoenix-like resurrection. Donny has custom-welded a complete new frame. Rather than try to find a working Model T engine, the plan is to hide a new four-cylinder gas engine and related modern works under the hood. The original went through multiple engine failures because with the nose up in the air, lubricating oil drained away from the first cylinder.

One practical question—how do you steer a car when the front wheels are up in the air? Our own Leapin' Lena lacked this option, but other versions had separate hand-levered brakes on each rear wheel. With this modification, a skilled driver could go straight, weave from side to side and even do pirouettes.

Maynard's Many High Schools, 1871–2014

The school that opened for the 2013–14 school year replaced the building next door, the one that had served as Maynard's high school from 1964 to 2013. The high school before that one had served for forty-eight years; hopes are that the newly constructed Maynard High School will outlast the two previous incarnations.

If not, we need to be aware of a mathematical oddity. The Summer Street high school building cost $61,000 in 1916. Roughly fifty years later, the replacement school cost twenty-five times as much, and fifty years later the new school cost twenty-five times as much as that one. This suggests that in 2063, Maynard's next high school will cost more than $1 billion!

The last school had a troubled gestation. In 1961, the town vote was against building a new high school. This was shortsighted, as the existing school had an official maximum capacity of 350 students (already exceeded), no library and a too-small gym. One year later, the vote went the other way, in favor of spending up to $1.7 million to go forward. The project was way overdue. Projections based on the baby boom were that the high school population would swell to 600 in ten years. And in truth, it hit 644 in 1971. Junior high school students were already on split sessions due to overcrowding, and the elementary schools were averaging 30 to 35 students per classroom. The new school relieved overcrowding across the entire school system.

A final photo of the sign that had adorned the old Maynard High School before it was demolished in the summer of 2013.

The class of 1965 was the first to graduate from the school building that just met its demise. Joseph Mullin was the class president of 124 graduating students. The class motto was "Non est vivere est valere vita," which translates to "Not merely to exist, but to amount to something in life."

As for the newest iteration of Maynard High School, the sixth to serve that function since the town was incorporated in 1871, construction broke ground in 2011. Classes began with the 2013–14 school year, even though the building and landscape were still works in progress.

Enrollment at Maynard High School ebbed from that 1970s peak of more than 600 to numbers in the low 300s for the last ten years, resulting in graduating classes of about 70 students. There has been a recent uptick in enrollment, but it is still small compared to our neighbors. Acton-Boxborough graduates 450 to 500 each year. Nashoba (serving Stow, Bolton and Lancaster) graduates about half that number. To the south, Lincoln-Sudbury sees off about 400 each year, while eastward, Concord-Carlisle says goodbye to approximately 325 seniors. What all ten towns share in common is that the great majority of their graduates go on to further education.

One bit of history many current residents are unaware of is that Alumni Field became the school's sports site some thirty-six years before the just-demolished school was built. In 1928, while Maynard High School was still at the Summer Street location, the town transferred the land that had been the Town (Poor) Farm meadow to the school department. The football team started using the new playing field for the 1928 season. Within a handful of years, Alumni Field gained a cinder track around the playing field, bleachers, hockey rink, field house and tennis courts.

At the time of the incorporation of Maynard in 1871, the new town was served by ten teachers working in four small school buildings. Salaries were in the range of nine to fifteen dollars a week (men were paid more than women). Nason Street School became the first high school, with a total enrollment of thirty-five students. Six years later, a new school was built on Acton Street. The high school moved back to the Nason Street site and then to Summer Street before decamping to the south side of town.

Table IV

LIST OF THE HIGH SCHOOLS

Nason Street	1871–1877
Acton Street	1877–1992
Nason Street	1892–1916
Summer Street	1916–1964
Maynard HS	1964–2013
Maynard HS	2013 to present

The third high school served from 1892 to 1916. This was a newly built wooden, twelve-room schoolhouse at the current site of the Maynard Public Library. The school suffered a minor fire on September 12, 1916, and then burned completely on September 20. Both fires were thought to be arson. The graduating class of 1892 decided on school colors of orange and black. Back then, the state required only that students remain in school until they were fourteen years old (changed to sixteen years in 1913), and only after 1898 were children under fourteen prohibited from factory work. The numbers of children actually finishing four years of high school were very small—the class of 1904 had only one!

The fourth high school was in the building currently occupied by ArtSpace. Construction was completed in time for the start of the 1916–17 school year. The school was nameless until 1932, when "Maynard High School" was approved at a town meeting vote. A timeline compiled by Ralph Sheridan and David Griffin noted, among these many facts, that football was reestablished as a school team for the fall of 1917, after a twelve-year hiatus. The team lost the first game, fifty-nine to zero. The school band got its start in 1933.

The Town Seal: Why Is the Time 12:10?

Anyone entering Maynard on Routes 62 or 117 passes a white sign with the words "Entering Maynard" framing a blue circle. Inside the circle is an image of a standing Native American on a shield; above the shield is a crest of an arm holding a sword. The figure holds a bow in one hand and an arrow pointing toward the ground in the other.

This raises the question: why did the town of Maynard vote for a Native American for a symbol? The answer: it did not. The same icon is on the other side of the sign, the one reading "Entering Stow" (or Sudbury, or Acton). What all these signs bear is actually the coat of arms of the Commonwealth of Massachusetts.

The charter to establish the Massachusetts Bay Colony, granted by King Charles I in 1629, authorized a seal that featured a semi-naked Indian holding a bow and arrow, with a speech balloon containing the words "Come over and help us" streaming from his mouth. (We all know how that worked out.)

This seal was discontinued around 1692, when the Massachusetts Bay Colony charter was annulled and the territory reorganized as the Province of Massachusetts Bay, without its own coat of arms or seal. So matters stood until the American Revolutionary War (1775–83).

The British abandoned Massachusetts years before the war ended. While war still raged uncertain to the south, the former Massachusetts Colony approved a state constitution in 1780 and decided it wanted its own seal. Nathan Cushing provided the revised design. His idea: go back to the original, lose the slogan, keep the Indian. After approval by Governor John Hancock, Paul Revere was commissioned to engrave the seal; his original bill for the work is on file at the Massachusetts State Archives.

The downward-pointing arrow signifies peaceful intent; the sword, the ongoing war. The Latin motto translates to "By the sword we seek peace, but peace only under liberty." Thus, the image as a whole is intended as a reminder that liberty was achieved through the American Revolution.

Wait, wait—but what about Maynard's original seal, approved at a town meeting in February 1889? In a word—uninspired. The original image

Maynard's town seal, 1889–1975, as printed on a ribbon for the centennial celebration in 1971. *Ribbon in collection of Maynard Historical Society.*

was one circle inside another. The outer border read, "Town of Maynard Massachusetts." The inner circle held: "Incorporated 1871."

The old town seal was replaced in January 1975. Maynard made this change four years after the Clock Tower was featured on the town centennial coin. Gerard D'Errico won the contest in 1971 for best design for the commemorative coin and was doubly honored when his design was chosen to replace the old town emblem.

D'Errico was a graphic artist and design engineer by trade. He served for years in the Maynard Fire Department and also in the U.S. Air Force Reserves. He passed away in 2009, survived by his wife, Patricia; son, John; daughter, Marianne; and an extended, multigenerational family.

The motto on the town seal is "Progressus cum Stabilitate," intended to translate from the Latin as "Progress with Stability." D'Errico's centennial coin design read, "Progressus cum Stabilitas." "Stabilitate" is the ablative singular form of "stabilitas." According to Latin scholars, the former is correct when following a preposition such as "cum." The Town of Maynard is of two minds. Official town documents bear the town seal with "Stabilitate," as do the newer street signs, but town-owned vehicles with the seal on the door have it as "Stabilitas," as does the sign outside the police station. Well, as they say in Latin, "Quicquid." (Whatever.)

The clock on the town of Maynard's seal shows the time as 12:10. Ten minutes after noon is when the fire station sounds its rooftop horn—audible throughout much of Maynard. Why 12:10 and not noon is shrouded in the mystery of history. Some say the answer is as simple as that, back in the day when the woolen mill sounded its noon steam whistle to announce lunch break, the fire department decided to offset its own by ten minutes so the two could never be confused.

Others say that the person in charge of the daily test would walk up to the train station to get the official time via telegraph, set his watch accordingly and then walk back to the firehouse. As the walk to the fire station, then on Nason Street, was just under ten minutes, the decision was made to be consistent about sounding the horn at 12:10.

Town records favor the latter explanation. Back in 1897, when the fire signal was a battery-triggered release of a striker hitting the school bell, budget accounts show William W. Oliver, who owned a jewelry shop next to the fire station, being paid twelve dollars per year for managing the daily test—at 12:10. The tradition continued after switching to a steam whistle at the mill and then to a compressed air horn atop the fire station. Given that the woolen mill closed in 1950 and the train station ten years later, it has to

Maynard's town seal from 1975 to present, based on Gerard D'Errico's design for the 1971 commemorative coin issued to honor Maynard's centennial.

be some combination of nostalgia and inertia that preserves the tradition long after the reasons are gone.

It's just as well that the Maynard town seal now features the town's iconic image. Starting in 2009, the State of Massachusetts decreed that most street signs change from the old standard of four-inch-tall lettering to versions with six-inch letters, with the option of including a pictograph, such as a town seal, to the left of the lettering.

To the east, Concord's seal features the minuteman statue and the motto "Quam firma res Concordia," loosely translated as "What a strong thing is harmony," with a play on words in "concordia." To the north, Acton's seal features an image of the Civil War monument, no motto. To the west, Stow's seal features the Randall Library, no motto. And to the south, Sudbury's seal features the Wadsworth Monument (honoring Samuel Wadsworth and others who died in battle in King Philip's War, 1876), again, no motto. Only in Concord and Maynard does it help to have a bit of Latin.

Movie Theaters: Colonial, Riverside, Peoples and Fine Arts

The first showing of a motion picture in Maynard was at the Riverside co-op (now the site of the Knights of Columbus building) in 1902. There is also mention of a 1909 exhibition of Sherman's moving pictures at the same place. Newspapers of that era mentioned S.E. Sherman as a have-projector-will-travel impresario. By 1914, there were occasional showing of features, shorts and newsreels at Colonial Hall. These were silent films in black and white, often accompanied by live music, typically a solo pianist. Intermissions featured performances by local singers.

The first location with regularly scheduled movie showings was Colonial Hall, the second story of 65–69 Main Street, in business from 1916 onward. Bartholomew "BJ" Coughlin was one of the owners. Riverside Theatre (then the second floor of what is now Gruber Bros. Furniture) started showing movies in 1922, run by Samuel Lerer. Riverside's run ended with a fire in 1934. The Colonial was still in business as late as 1952. Nine cents got you in, and one penny bought candy.

The first building specifically designed to serve as a motion picture palace was Peoples Theatre. The building still stands at 14 Nason Street, converted to office space. Initially, two groups of local businessmen were scrambling for downtown locations and funding. James A. Coughlan, Hector Hobers and James J. Ledgart organized the Peoples Theatre Company and sold shares for twenty-five dollars. The co-operative movement was very strong in Maynard at the time, so the idea of local people being able to buy into ownership and share the profits was well received. In fact, the decision to go for crowd-sourced funding was instrumental to choosing the theater's name.

The second group (BJ Coughlin, the Naylor brothers and others) had land at the corner of Nason and Main Streets but not quite enough money. The two groups merged. Peoples Theatre opened on May 6, 1921, with seating for 700 people (250 in the balcony). A huge chandelier graced the lobby.

During the first half of the twentieth century, local businesses often sponsored sports teams for publicity purposes. At Peoples Theatre, Burton Coughlan (in suit) managed the team. He was thirty-four at the time. His father was one of the investors who started Peoples. *Courtesy of Maynard Historical Society.*

Tickets were twenty-five cents. In 1951, the price of a ticket was up to forty-four cents for adults and sixteen cents for children. The theater closed its doors after a nearly forty-year run.

Although the Coughlans, father James and son Burton, were involved with Peoples, Burton decided to build his own theater on the family property at 19 Summer Street. His vision, the luxuriously appointed Fine Arts Theatre, with four hundred seats and no balcony, opened on June 29, 1949, with a showing of *The Red Shoes.* An adjoining second theater, with three hundred seats and its own ticket window, was added in 1969. One employee reminisced, "The projectionist had to scamper across the roof to get to the [projection] booth for the smaller of the theaters." That theater was divided into two parts in 1989.

Over decades, Fine Arts lost it lustre (and much of its heat, air conditioning, sound-system and waterproofing) until, by the beginnings of this century, it

James T. Coughlan opened Coughlan's Livery in 1897, converted the business to an auto shop around 1913 and then, in collaboration with his son, opened the Fine Arts Theatre in 1949. Linda Coughlan Flint, Burton's daughter, sold the theater to Steven Trumble in 2013. Photo taken February 2011.

was a mess of threadbare carpets, duct-taped seats and sad bathrooms. The Shea family, operating as Deco Entertainment Services, leased the property in late 2002 and started a lengthy rehab process on the interior. Then, in 2013, Burton Coughlan's daughter sold the theater plus the building at 17 Summer Street (originally part of the stables, later Burton's art gallery) to the partnership of Steven Trumble and Melanie Perry.

Their extensive rehabilitation process, outside and inside, has taken far more money and time than initially expected, including half a year with closed doors and dark screens. Trumble swears that during the remodeling process they excavated and renovated through layers upon layers of movie theater detritus, auto body shop and, finally, down to the wooden timbers and square-cut nails. So all the more sweet that sixty-five years after its premiere, the Fine Arts Theatre had a grand reopening in June 2014.

5
UNUSUAL BUSINESSES

M ost New England cities and towns have had their share of businesses that elicit a sense of "You're kidding, right?" when mentioned in today's conversations. Maynard may have had more than its share.

Funeral Homes and Cemeteries

Until the beginnings of the twentieth century, embalming was a relatively rare practice. People tended to die where they lived and be buried—fairly quickly—in the town where they died. There was a spate of embalming during the Civil War, primarily conducted by military surgeons on officers who died in battle or from wounds or illness behind the battle lines and whose families wanted them returned for burial in the local cemetery. This practice fell out of favor after the war.

Instead, the undertaker—a man whose business was to "undertake" all arrangements for funerals—would come to the family home to prepare the body. Burials were for the immediate family and local community. Over time, customs changed; with the telegraph and trains, distantly located relatives would expect to learn of a death in the family and could attend the funeral. Embalming allowed for more time between death and interment. By the early to mid-1920s, the funeral home as we know it was beginning to emerge—with back rooms for the preparation of bodies and front rooms for gatherings of family and friends to pay their last respects to the guest of honor.

In the early 1900s, the Maynard Hebrew Society invited a rabbi to conduct Sabbath services in rented meeting halls. In September 1921, the congregation established Rodoff Shalom Synagogue in a house on Acton Street (next to where Avis car rentals is now). The congregation was active to 1980, when it merged with the newly formed Congregation Beth Elohim in Acton. In a temple newsletter, Adam Jacoby remembered, "In 1980 we built a new building and marched the Torah from Maynard to Acton under a chuppa with shofars blowing. I was one of the shofrot during the walk." *Photo from 1970, courtesy of Maynard Historical Society.*

Henry Fowler—a signer of the 1871 petition to create the town of Maynard—was an undertaker. His son, Orrin S. Fowler, followed in the family business in 1887. Orrin and his wife, Nellie, were a power couple. He was on the founding boards of banks and held many town government offices. She was a member of the Daughters of the American Revolution and the first president of the American Legion Ladies Auxiliary. They were among the honorables on the very first electric trolley ride in 1901. Their son, Guyer Fowler (Harvard graduate, class of 1915, and World War I veteran who served in France), followed in the family business until his death in 1956, at age sixty-three. Fowler-Kennedy Funeral Service, Inc., on Concord Street, was started by Guyer and his business partner

Orrin Fowler was in the undertaker's trade, just like his father, as shown in an advertisement from the 1887 town directory. *Courtesy of Maynard Historical Society.*

at that location in 1941. This is the sole representative of the funeral business in Maynard today.

At one time, there were four. Herbert Martin started in 1927. Years later, his son-in-law, John Doran, joined the business, making it the Martin & Doran Funeral Home, which later moved to Acton. Sheehan and White Funeral Home operated on Bancroft Street into the 1970s. The W.A. Twombly Funeral Home had started out on Main Street near the Methodist church before relocating to 42 Summer Street and then closing in the 1950s.

Prior to the founding of Maynard, the dead would have been buried in Sudbury or Stow. But with the start of church congregations in what was known as Assabet Village and the sense of becoming a community, people wanted to be buried closer to their families. Part of what is now Glenwood Cemetery was in use as a burial ground as far back as the 1850s. The first occupant after the cemetery was formally dedicated in 1871 was Thomas H. Brooks. St. Bridget's Cemetery also got off to an informal start, as a man named O'Donnell was planted in 1859, a decade before James Heffernan officially reached six feet under. Both cemeteries are still active.

Counting the Dead

How many people are buried in Maynard? Roughly 11,500. So for one thing, the dead outnumber the living. This fact is not true for the neighboring towns, which despite having been in existence two hundred years longer came to their current larger populations late.

This estimate comes from a combination of asking and counting and guessing. The records for St. Bridget's Cemetery are fairly good. The church's count is about 4,800. Town records for Glenwood Cemetery are incomplete. Rumor has it that some were used in the cemetery shed's pot-bellied stove as fire starters. Peg Brown, one of Maynard's self-appointed amateur historians, took up the project of counting the dead. Her unofficial database—compiled from official records and headstone readings—lists 6,766 names along with section and lot numbers, plus year of death for the great majority.

Another way to approach this is as a math problem. Down the decades, the U.S. census provided population counts and mortality rates (as deaths per thousand per year). Prior to 1850, the death rate for Massachusetts was

This crypt facing Route 27 is mysteriously marked "1888" rather than with a family name. It turns out that the town built this as a "temporary" to hold coffins for the time it took to dig a grave. Blocks of ice were brought in to keep bodies cold if frozen ground made for slow digging.

about 25 per 1,000 and perhaps higher in urban, immigrant-populated areas. Children died. Women died. Men died. For those who made it past their harrowing first five years, average lifespan was fifty-five years. Cleaner water, safer food and vaccinations brought the state's rate down to 15 per 1,000 by one hundred years ago. Modern medicine and a decline in tobacco use have us at today's rate of 8 per 1,000. Multiplying population for each decade by estimated death rate per decade and adding all that up results in a total of 11,300. This is quite close to the combined counts by Ms. Brown and St. Bridget Roman Catholic Church.

A third way is to page through the town's annual reports, which list deaths for each year from 1880 to 2012. A note to future historians: from 1880 through 1927, the records listed the dead by name and provided cause of death. From this, we learn that in the last few months of 1918, the influenza epidemic took thirty-five people of all ages. Life was more at risk in general. Barely a year went by without a railroad-related death, an accidental drowning, a suicide or a mill accident. Noted, but less frequently occurring, causes included death from burns, poisonings and murders.

Tallying up deaths and adding an estimate for the undocumented early years results in a total of 11,100. Using this approach to estimate burials ignores those who died here but were buried elsewhere and also those who died elsewhere and were buried here (perhaps balancing each other). Since 1985, the percent of cremations has increased dramatically, from 15 percent then to 40 percent now, and this, too, adds uncertainty to equated deaths to burials. Still, all three methods converge on a total between 11,100 and 11,500.

Going forward, hope is that a person as dedicated as Peg Brown will create a database and map for St. Bridget's Cemetery and also keep Glenwood Cemetery records current. For it's an embarrassment to lose track of the dead. (After all, they aren't going anywhere.) In 2012, Sudbury brought in ground-penetrating radar and tentatively identified 957 unrecorded graves. Stow's historians suspect hundreds are undocumented in the Lower Village Cemetery. Back to the original question: how many people are buried in Maynard's cemeteries? The answer: all of them.

The Gunpowder Mills on Powder Mill Road

Ka-boom! There was a 105-year history of gunpowder manufacture in this area. A 1921 history of Maynard noted that many local men found

Addison O. Fay was president of American Powder Mills. His father, Addison G. Fay, died in an explosion in 1873. *Courtesy of Maynard Historical Society.*

employment in the American Powder Mills, adding, "occasional explosions, sometimes serious, do not permit us to ignore their [APM's] existence." A newspaper account of an explosion on March 12, 1878, described widely scattered body parts of two workers being gathered in pails, including a detached finger bearing a gold ring. The location of this spread-out complex was along what is now Route 62, encompassing parts of Maynard, Acton, Concord and Sudbury on both sides of the Assabet River.

The black powder manufacturing process, in brief: potassium nitrate, sulfur and softwood charcoal are each milled separately to a fine powder and then mixed together while dampened with water. The blend is pressed to remove water and the presscake then broken into the desired coarseness (for cannons) or fineness (for guns) in the kernel-house and sieved to remove dust, with the resulting grains glazed with graphite to prevent sticking, dried and then packed into copper-nailed oak barrels or tin containers. Because of the dangerous nature of gunpowder, this type of operation was typically composed of modest-sized wooden buildings quite a distance apart from one another.

Thoreau's journal mentions the gunpowder mills several times. Passing by on an 1851 walk to Lake Boon, Thoreau complained that the harsh chemicals irritated his throat. Later the same year, he recounted having asked a worker about the dangers of working with gunpowder. Per his journal, the workmen wore shoes without iron tacks so as to reduce the risk of striking a spark. The workers considered the kernel-house the most dangerous, the drying-house next and the press-house next. Two years after Thoreau's first journal entries, there was an explosion at the mill. Thoreau wrote:

About ten minutes before 10 a.m. I heard a very loud sound and felt a violent jar which made the house rock and the loose articles on my table rattle. I jumped into a man's wagon and rode toward the mills. Arrived probably before half past 10:00 a.m. There were perhaps 30 or 40 wagons there. The kernel mill had blown up first and killed three men who were in it said to be turning a roller with a chisel…and fragments mostly but a foot or two in length were strewn over the hills and meadows, as if sown, for 30 rods [165 yards]. Three other buildings were destroyed or damaged.

Some of the clothes of the men were in the tops of the trees where undoubtedly their bodies had been and left them. The bodies were naked and black. Some limbs and bowels here and there, and a head at a distance from its trunk. The feet were bare, the hair singed to a crisp. I smelt the powder half a mile before I got there.

Henry David Thoreau was rubbernecking at the site of the gunpowder mills that Nathan Pratt built in 1835. Previously, a dam at that site had provided power for a sawmill. Pratt had learned his trade at the gunpowder mills in Barre, Massachusetts. That operation became incorporated as the Massachusetts Powder Works, which then bought Pratt's business in 1864, moved its own equipment to Pratt's site because his was close to a railroad and then took on his company's name: American Powder Company. Under subsequent ownerships by the American Powder Mills (1883–1929) and American Cyanamid Company (1929–1940), the operation grew to some forty buildings scattered over 401 acres—mostly in Acton and Maynard—employing at times as many as sixty men and a dozen or more women (the latter to assemble cartridges). The company had its own small-gauge railroad to carry freight to and from the railroad a mile north.

Descriptions of the time mention willow tree wood being brought in from Sudbury to make the charcoal and unshod mules being used to pull wagons within the mill compound because of the fear that horseshoe-shod horses might strike sparks. Coming off work, men would leave their gunpowder-soiled clothing in the changing room and wash thoroughly before changing into clean clothes to go home.

American Powder Mills added production of smokeless powder, including the renowned brand Dead Shot, but continued making black powder. Interestingly, during World War I, the facility's entire production was contracted to the Russian government. And why wasn't it selling to the United States? Because DuPont had an exclusive contract.

The first fatal explosion mentioned in historic records occurred in 1836. The *Concord Freeman* reported that three men were blown to bits, and a fourth succumbed hours later to burns and fractures. Various records documented twenty-three explosions—many with fatalities. A *New York Times* article told

This granite millstone lies partially buried about fifteen yards from the remnants of what appears to be an explosion-wracked mill building. The stone's dimensions are fifty-eight inches in diameter by sixteen inches thick, with an estimated weight of four thousand pounds.

of five deaths in a multi-building series of explosions on May 3, 1898. A September 4, 1915 explosion was heard as far away as Lowell and Boston. The last three explosions on record took place in 1940; the mills were closed shortly thereafter.

Soon after gunpowder manufacture ceased, ownership of most of the land devolved to W.R. Grace, an international chemical company, and later still was sold off to various business sites such as the Stop & Shop Plaza and car-related businesses on both sides of Powder Mill Road. Remnants of gunpowder mill buildings can be seen on forays into the woods. The dam still exists, with an adjoining, recently modernized hydroelectric facility operating under the name Acton Hydro Company. Electricity is sold to customers of Concord's municipal power company.

Maydale Beverage Company

Maynard's one-time bustling soda company, epitomized by the very popular Maydale Ginger Ale, ceased operations in the mid-1960s. The customer list was sold to Chelmsford Ginger Ale, at that time a division of Canada Dry Ginger Ale. The term "dry" in this context means a milder ginger taste and lower sugar content than was typical of the traditional (now rare) golden ginger ale.

The ingredients listed on a Maydale Ginger Ale label would fit right in with today's bias for simplicity. Note no high fructose corn syrup (not invented yet). Modern products add sodium benzoate—a preservative—and are coy about the exact nature of flavoring, typically listed as "natural flavors." This means no synthetic ginger flavor, but many mainstream ginger ales contain lemon and lime flavors, and sometimes pineapple, honey and various spices, in addition to ginger.

Maynard's soda business originated with Waino Keto owning and operating Maynard Bottling Works on Euclid Avenue. He started the business in 1899. Returnable glass bottles were washed, rinsed, filled, capped and labeled by hand. Production was a few dozen cases per week. Karl Paul Hilander, who went by the name K. Paul Hilander, started working for Keto in 1913 and then bought the company in early 1914. A year later, he relocated to Glendale Street at a site that had access to spring water.

Immigration records indicate that Hilander was born in 1889 in Bjarnbarg, Finland. He immigrated to the United States in 1908 and became a citizen in 1921. Somewhere along the way, his name morphed from Helander to

Maydale's brightly colored robin logo was on every bottle label and stenciled onto every wooden case. Maydale offered eight-ounce bottles when Coca-Cola bottles were six and a half ounces. *Courtesy of Maynard Historical Society.*

the perhaps more American-sounding Hilander. What's missing from this story is where, at age twenty-four, he got the money not only to buy the soda company but also to buy out the Cullen Wet Wash Laundry that had been operating at the Glendale site. One possibility is the money came from his wife's family, as her maiden name was Keto; it's possible she was related to Waino Keto, the original owner.

In 1916, Hilander decided on the name Maydale, from combining Maynard with Glendale. His businesses provided spring water as the Maydale Spring Company and bottled soda as the Maydale Beverage Co., Inc. In addition to ginger ale, flavors included root beer, birch beer, sarsaparilla and orange.

At its peak, Maydale was the bottled beverage of choice in Maynard and surrounding towns as far away as Fitchburg. Production topped thousands of cases per week. A nickel would buy an eight-ounce bottle. The clear glass bottles are not infrequent finds whenever people dig on their property to put in gardens or paths. Hilander had between twelve and fifteen people working for him, including drivers for his delivery trucks.

Hilander owned the business into the 1950s. He and his wife, Helmi (also an immigrant from Finland), both died in 1959 and are buried in Glenwood Cemetery. The gravestone also names Norman (1913–1914) and Kenneth (1916–1919), their children.

The soda and spring water business continued for a while under Arnold Anderson, until he converted the site to an auto body shop for his Ford dealership (where the Avis car rental site is now). The Maydale building still stands, behind 25 Glendale Street, but perhaps not for long, as it is definitely showing age.

Today's ginger ale products are not what they used to be. Modern ginger beer (confusingly, a nonalcoholic product) is closer in nature to the old stuff. More than two dozen companies offer a wide range of choices in ginger beer, from mild to having a fiery bite. A popular mixed drink—a Dark and Stormy—combines ginger beer and dark rum. A shandy is traditionally half beer and half lemonade or ginger beer. Historically, the golden age for old-recipe ginger ale was Prohibition (1919–33) because speakeasies found that in a mixed drink, the strong taste of ginger would mask the off-tastes of bootleg-quality liquor.

Taylor's Mink Ranch

Older residents of Maynard remember when the town had a mink farm (not unique to the area—Sudbury had three). What was the Taylor farm is now the site of the senior housing complex on Concord Street Circle, off Concord Street, east of Route 27.

Town directories from the 1920s onward list John W. Taylor as a fur dealer living at 60 Concord with his wife, Hulda. Townspeople remember the Taylors' farm as still in operation into the 1960s. George Walls recalled, "As kids, we would sneak over there to see the minks in rows of small cages. The smell from all the feces and urine dripping through the wire mesh was horrible."

Typically, a mink farm, or "ranch" in the parlance of the day, would have had one thousand to five thousand mink in individual cages under long, open-sided sheds. Each wire mesh cage was about twenty by twenty by thirty inches, with the bottoms thirty inches above ground. Each year started with breeding animals in early March, followed by births of four to eight kits per litter in May. Come November, most of the mink were killed and skinned at the farm. The remaining 20 percent were overwintered to be breeding stock for the next year.

Food was mostly byproducts from chicken slaughterhouses, run through a meat grinder. Keep in mind that many of the towns located between what are now Interstates 95 and 495 were no more than scantily populated areas dominated by fruit orchards and chicken farms.

Fur farming in the United States consolidated over time. Many farmers "pelted out" in the 1960s—i.e., killed all their animals and got out of the business—as a combination of lowering demand and increased foreign production made mink farming only marginally profitable. Today, there are only about 275 active mink farm operations in the United States. However, average size increased over time to more than ten thousand animals, and profits have recently skyrocketed. New farms are being started. Mink farms of this size are spread out over twenty acres or more, surrounded by security fences and guarded by alarm systems.

China leads the world in mink farming, with 25 percent of world production plus a fast-growing demand for mink coats among the new middle and upper classes. In fact, demand has grown to the point that top-quality pelts from America, which just a few years ago went for $40 each, now fetch about $100. Buyers, who were predominantly Jewish merchants from New York's garment industry fifty years ago, are now mostly Chinese or Russian. All this means the U.S. production of three million pelts a year is worth on the upside of $300 million.

John Taylor was more than a mere mink farmer. As a furrier with a store in Boston, he partnered with Percy V. Noble, a Canadian mink rancher. Together they turned a fortuitous color mutation that had occurred in Noble's breeding stock in 1937 into the first ever offering of natural white mink. This was just after the end of World War II.

Sonja Henie, the famous Norwegian Olympic figure skater and later ice show and movie star, was one of the early wearers of Noble-Taylor white mink coats and also incorporated white mink into skating outfits for her ice-skating shows. One of her mink coats was valued at $20,000 back when a new car cost around $1,500.

John W. Taylor was a marine sharpshooter in World War I. His name is on the World War I plaque in Memorial Park. Wounded in the war, he recovered to return stateside and was assigned to Liberty Bond

Percy V. Noble, Sonja Heine and John W. Taylor, all three holding white mink pelts that would go into making Sonja's famous white mink coat. *Courtesy of Maynard Historical Society.*

fundraising events, touring the country by train with Douglas Fairbanks and Mary Pickford.

According to Frederick Johnson of Maynard, whose sister was married to Taylor's son, Taylor's interest in furs began after the war with his buying pelts from local trappers. He subsequently opened up a furrier's on Washington Street, in Boston, and became known for offering high-quality fur coats. He was notorious for buying only top-quality pelts at the annual auctions in New York City.

In time, he started breeding mink on his property along Concord Street. As Fred tells it, "Mr. Taylor and his wife, Hulda, had a huge mink ranch—maybe as many as ten thousand animals. He was an expert on the rare, light-colored fur mutations. What he did not raise on his ranch he got from Percy Noble, his Canadian partner."

As for what the mink were fed, Fred went on to recount, "Any time a horse died in Maynard, south Acton or Stow, one of Taylor's employees would go round with a wagon. The carcasses would be processed for food."

Mink escape mink farms all the time. After more than one hundred generations in captivity, selective breeding has resulted in animals almost twice the size of their wild relatives (for larger pelts) but oddly with smaller brains. One theory is this is a result of selecting for animals that will tolerate being confined in small cages. Researchers estimate that more than 90 percent of escaped or deliberately released mink die within two months. The few that survive can either mate with native mink or form a feral population. North American mink are now considered an invasive species in Europe, northern Asia and the southern end of South America.

Locally, there is evidence of past escapes from Taylor's mink ranch. Fifty years after the Taylor ranch closed, there are still documented sightings of an occasional white mink at Concord's Great Meadow National Wildlife Refuge.

Powell Flutes

An inverted triangle logo and "Powell Flutes" grace the end of the Clock Tower building closest to the Farmers' Market parking lot. The triangle displays the stylized letters VQP for Verne Q. Powell, the founder of the company.

According to postings at powellflutes.com and flutebuilder.com, Powell was a jeweler and engraver living in Fort Scott, Kansas. He came from a musical family and played piccolo and flute (wooden) in the town band. During a visit to Chicago, he heard a European flutist performing on a silver flute. He was so impressed with the quality of the sound that he decided to craft a silver flute. As the story goes, he melted silver coins, watch cases

The Powell Flutes sign faces the parking lot where the Farmers' Market sets up every summer weekend, yet few people know what goes on inside.

and teaspoons to make the first silver flute in America in 1910. The keys were inlaid with gold from gold coins. The instrument became known as the "Spoon Flute" and is still in the family's possession to this day.

This flute came to the attention of William S. Haynes, one of several wind instrument makers based in Boston. Haynes hired Powell as foreman, and he worked there for over ten years before setting out on his own in 1927. Powell's shop was on Huntington Avenue, near the New England Conservatory of Music and Boston Symphony Hall.

From the beginning, Powell flutes and piccolos were renowned as top-quality professional instruments. Still, the business grew slowly. It took twenty-five years to reach flute number one thousand. Verne Q. Powell sold the company to a group of employees in 1961 and retired in early 1962. He was eighty-two years old at the time and stopped making flutes only because he had broken his right hand in a fall. Powell died in 1968. After his death, the company moved from Boston to Arlington in 1970 and then to Waltham in 1989.

Powell Flutes is currently owned by Steven Wasser, a graduate of Harvard Business School. He bought into the company in 1986, bought out the other co-owner in 1989 and then moved the company to Maynard in 1999. Under his management, Powell continues to innovate at all levels, while having also launched a lower-cost line of instruments to complement the higher-priced brands and custom-made flutes. Powell Flutes employs about fifty people.

When asked why musical instruments, Mr. Wasser answered, "It was a happy accident. I was looking to purchase a business. My family has a long musical history, and I myself play clarinet. My accountant also handled accounting for Powell Flutes and mentioned that the company might be looking for an investor."

And as for why he chose Maynard: "I was looking for a building with history, situated amidst a community, rather than a modern building surrounded by parking lots."

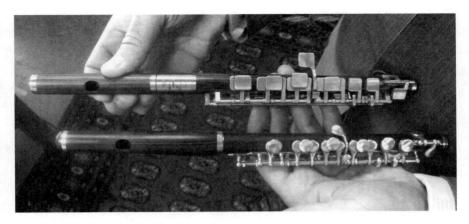

Steven Wasser, president and owner of Powell Flutes, held a new model piccolo with ergonomically designed stainless steel keys (top) and a traditional model with sterling silver keys (bottom).

Rebecca Weissman, communications manager, added, "The flutes and piccolos are made here. We believe that Powell Flutes is the only company at Clock Tower Place that is involved in actual manufacture rather than just office operations."

Eastern Massachusetts is a nexus of American flute manufacture. The William S. Haynes Company, from which Verne Q. Powell had left to start his own company, still exists and, much like Powell Flutes, exited Boston after many years in the city. Haynes is now located in Acton. The Brannen brothers left Powell in 1977 to make flutes on their own and are currently in Woburn. Lillian Burkart and Jim Phelan met while working at Powell, married and later launched Burkart Flutes & Piccolos, currently in Shirley. Di Zhao worked for Powell and then Haynes before starting Di Zhao Flutes in Westford.

There's more. David Williams was at Powell, put in a stint at Brannen Brothers and, in 1990, launched Williams Flutes in Arlington. Lev Levit followed the same Powell-to-Brannen path before starting Levit Flute Company in Natick. Kanichi Nagahara started in flutes in Japan and then put in a few years at two Boston-area flute companies (coyly, his website does not name names) before starting Nagahara Flutes, now in Chelmsford.

A Powell flute (#365) commanded the highest price ever paid for a flute. This platinum flute with a sterling silver mechanism was commissioned for an exhibit at the 1939 World's Fair in New York. In 1986, the same flute was auctioned at Christie's for $187,000. For a time, it was on display at the Metropolitan Museum of Art.

Lastly, a Powell flute has journeyed into space. Massachusetts resident astronaut Catherine "Cady" Coleman had three trips into space over the period from 1995 to 2011. Her last was a 159-day stint in the Space Station. Included in the personal belongings each Space Station inhabitant is allowed was her handmade sterling silver flute. On April 11, 2011, she played a flute duet with Ian Anderson of the band Jethro Tull (she in space, he on earth and both on Powell flutes).

Northern Recording Studio

Once upon a time, gods and demigods of rock and roll walked the streets of Maynard. It was the '70s. Aerosmith, Talking Heads, the Cars, Tommy Bolin Band, Johnny Barnes, Thundertrain...all recorded at the Great Northern Studio, aka Northern Studio, Northern Recording Studio, Northern Sound or Northern Lights Recording Studio, located on the second floor of the brick building at 63 Main Street.

Back then, the Rathskeller—better known as "The Rat"—was a live music club in Kenmore Square, Boston. Many Massachusetts bands that came through there became almost famous. Some of those bands, when cutting demo tapes, recording songs, taping live radio shows or maybe just adding tracks to songs recorded elsewhere, often ended up in Maynard. The building itself has a long history. This upstairs space in Colonial Hall, which was built in 1914, served as one of Maynard's early movie theaters and also did duty as a dance hall and meeting room. Downstairs, Woolworths moved in with a small store in 1916, later expanding to the entire ground floor. One anecdote that connects the two comes from Joe Viglione's *History of New England Rock*: "Worcester/Boston radio station WAAF broadcast Duke & the Drivers live from Northern Sound on the day Elvis Presley died, August 16, 1977, with approximately one thousand people jammed into the studio atop a Woolworths five-and-dime"—likely a wildly exaggerated number but definitely crowded.

The Great Northern Studio was started by Peter Casperson and Bob Runstein, both out of Boston. Casperson is still very active in music management. Runstein's book, *Modern Recording Techniques*, now in its fifth edition, is considered the bible of the industry. Later, the studio was taken over by Bill Riseman and operated under the name Northern Studio.

And thus it was that up one long flight of steps, Thundertrain came to record songs for its first album, *Teenage Suicide*, including "Hot for Teacher!"

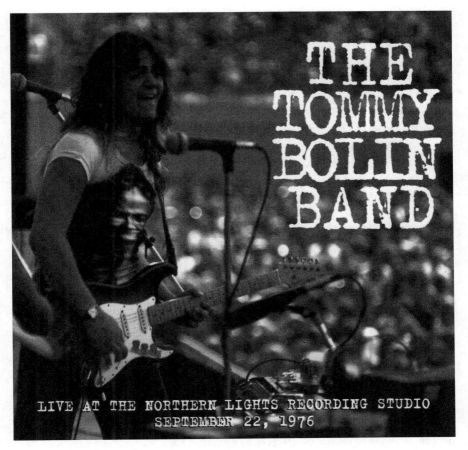

Tommy Bolin died in 1976, less than three months after this album was recorded as a live radio broadcast at Northern Studio. The CD (not issued until 1997) used a photo from an August 1976 concert. *Photo courtesy of Robert Ferbrache.*

(ten years before Van Halen's hit of the same name). Reddy Teddy taped its first album in 1976, as did the Earl Slick Band. The Tommy Bolin Band recorded "Live at Northern Lights" during a WBCN broadcast the same year.

One year later, the Cars did a demo tape of "Just What I Needed." Also in 1977, side one of *The Name of This Band Is Talking Heads* was recorded for a WCOZ radio broadcast but did not appear on that double album compilation until 1982.

Stories have it that many other bands recorded a track or two, or maybe an entire song or album, at Northern Studios through those years. One of the few that bothered to credit that in the liner notes was Boston, which, on the

1978 album *Don't Look Back*, acknowledged that the piano track on "A Man I'll Never Be" was recorded in Maynard. Researching obscure discographies added recording work done for Duke and the Drivers, James Montgomery Blues Band, Barbara Holliday, Cap'n Swing, Andy Pratt, Eastwood Peak, the Dawgs and the Blend. Some of this appeared on the Jelly Records label.

Life at the studio must have been interesting. This from a forum post on gearslutz.com: "The first time I ever saw a 'beer machine' [soda machine stocked with cans of beer] was at Northern Sound in Maynard, MA in the late '70s. I thought it was the coolest thing in the world!"

John Savignano was a student of Bob Runstein in Boston and was instrumental in getting the studio set up in Maynard. He served as assistant engineer for Peter and Bob and later for Bill Riseman. According to Savignano, Aerosmith was in for three nights doing some early rehearsal work on what became *Toys in the Attic*. "Having Aerosmith record in Maynard was very exciting, and as word slowly leaked out there was a steady stream of teenagers hanging around the back door. I say 'slowly leaked out' but I should say 'blasted out,' as even the acoustically insulated walls of the studio could not contain the ripping, thundering sounds of Aerosmith."

After Northern folded, some of Riseman's boards and other equipment ended up at the very successful Long View Farm Studios, in North Brookfield, Massachusetts. Riseman joined his father's business. William Riseman Associates was known for designing more movie theaters and multiplex theaters than any other architectural firm in America. He continued his father's line of work after his father's death and also became a leader in the architectural and archaeological use of virtual reality imagery. Riseman died in 1994.

6

UNUSUAL PEOPLE

S mall towns have characters. Cities have characters, too, but not known or known about by almost everyone in town. Here are portraits of a handful who were in one way or another notable.

Poet Laureate of Maynard

One hundred years ago, William C. Kenyon was locally known for poems published in the *Maynard News*. Kenyon worked at the woolen mill. Little is known about him. Apparently, he married Eva Wilson in 1895, lived in Maynard and then moved away in 1919. The newspaper published more than fifty of his poems over the period from 1913 to 1919. The Maynard Historical Society has on file a binder containing most of Kenyon's poems, transcribed from archived copies of the newspaper. Internet searches yield no additional information.

His topics were local (the woolen mill, a town election, the bandstand controversy) and also general (the war, death, motherhood). Quite a number of the poems had to do with efforts to ban the sale of alcohol. This was a topic Kenyon appeared ambivalent about, as in several poems he portrayed the harmful influence of alcohol, while in another he lamented Maynard voting itself dry. Here are excerpts from some of his poems (which will benefit from being read out loud). The first example is the beginning lines from "Maynard's Woolen Mill":

Upon the river Assabet,
which flows by Summer Hill,
in the old town of Maynard, Mass,
stands Maynard's woolen mill.
A high imposing structure,
the largest of its kind;
it answers well the purposes,
for which it was designed.
It is not a thing of beauty,
though planned with greatest skill;
it was ugly when completed,
and it is ugly still.

This one goes on for eight more verses of similar length. It was in print in 1918, about when the large new buildings closest to the millpond were being completed. The next is from "A Protest." Kenyon was castigating speculators who were driving up the price of food during the war:

And some of our men of finance,
if I had the proper dope,
should be made to do a high dance,
with their necks inside a rope.
For the men who rob our children,
of their meat and of their bread,
should be hung from some high building,
and left there till they're dead.

This one also had eight more verses in a similar vein. Kenyon's style was not concise. Most of his work fell into the range of three hundred to six hundred words. He tended to rhyme alternating lines—except when he didn't.

The next example: it's April 1915, and the town of Maynard had just voted itself dry. The neighboring towns were consistently dry, but Maynard flip-flopped from year to year. Prohibition was town-by-town, county-by-county or state-by-state before it became federal law in 1919. From the start of "The Wail of the Wets":

Yes, Maynard went dry, and we wonder why,
For no one seems to know.
Now, just how quick can we make the trip,

Thirsty men, hoping for a ride. *Drawing by Bruce Davidson, artist and owner of Serendipity Café.*

from here to Marlboro?
For spring is here and we want beer,
we don't care what you say.
So we ask you, what shall we do,
after the first of May?

One poem came to Maynard long after the Kenyons had moved away. In February 1938, he wrote "My Wife" in memory of his wife's recent death.

They had lived on the hill south of the mill, and he writes of the evenings the two of them had stepped out of their house to walk to the top of the hill to see the sunset. He concludes with the thought that as he closes his eyes to sleep, his wife, his mother and his many brothers and sisters who had predeceased him are watching over him.

Titanic Disaster Affected Local Resident

The RMS *Titanic* sank in 1912. According to accounts in the February 14, 1913 issues of the *Maynard News* and the *Concord Enterprise*, Frances M. Ford filed a lawsuit against the White Star Line for losses suffered in the disaster. Miss Ford had crossed the Atlantic in 1911. She found work as a domestic servant. Her letters to her family, with glowing accounts of the prospects of a good life in America, convinced them to make the crossing.

Back in England, Miss Ford's mother, Margaret Ann Watson Ford, sold the family's meager belongings and bought tickets for herself and her four other children: Dollina, age twenty; Edward, age eighteen; William, age fifteen; and Robina, age seven. Also crossing with the Ford family was Mrs. Ford's younger sister, Eliza Johnston; her husband, Andrew Johnston; and their two young children. In all, they were a party of nine. Their one-way tickets in third class cost a bit more than seven British pounds—roughly $400 per person in today's dollars.

None of the Fords or Johnstons survived. Miss Ford was living in New York at the time of the ship's sinking, but she became so despondent after her loss of nine family members that she gave up her position to go live with an uncle and aunt, Mr. and Mrs. Thomas Watson, in Haverhill, Massachusetts, later relocating with them to Maynard. It was while living in Maynard that Miss Ford made the local newspaper by deciding to join the many who were filing lawsuits against the White Star Line.

The sinking of the *Titanic* caused many wrongful death and loss of property lawsuits to be filed in the courts of the United States and United Kingdom. Claims filed in the United States alone easily exceeded $10 million. A legal definition of ownership of the *Titanic* would be crucial to remuneration.

The backstory: John Pierpont Morgan, a wealthy American, bought the White Star Line in 1902. A nuance of the purchase was that White Star continued to be registered as a British shipping company with British officers and crew, hence RMS *Titanic*, signifying Royal Mail Ship. By doing so, Morgan avoided enforcement of U.S. anti-monopoly laws.

There was another benefit. White Star claimed that the tragic loss occurred without any cause on its part and filed a petition to this effect asking for a cap on its liability based on the Limitation of Liability Act of 1851. The U.S. government had passed this law to make U.S. shipping more competitive via lower insurance costs. The law specified that damages could not exceed the value of the ship *at the end of the voyage in question*. Even if the ship was insured by the owner, the claimants had no claim to the insurance payout, only the ship's remaining value.

Nothing could be salvaged from the *Titanic*. Morgan argued that the remnant value of the *Titanic* was only $96,000—calculated from the value of the recovered lifeboats—thus leaving little to file lawsuits against.

Across the ocean, a British citizen counterclaimed that since the ship sailed under British registry, England's maritime law should apply to his lawsuit. Under this law, the liability limit would be determined by the size and value of the ship—in this case several million dollars. Morgan initially lost his petition for U.S. jurisdiction, appealed to the U.S. Supreme Court and won there. Thus, all successful lawsuits filed in the United States would divvy up only $96,000 (minus lawyers' fees). But because of the ship's registry, lawsuits could be brought in Britain and would have access to the larger pool of money.

History does not reveal if Miss Ford was successful in her lawsuit. On a different note, there was no mention of a Mr. Ford being on the *Titanic* with his wife and children, the reason being that he had deserted the family in 1904, shortly after the birth of their last child, leaving Margaret Ford to struggle in poverty as a single mother of five. However, he joined the British lawsuits against the White Star Line and was awarded a modest annuity.

Babe Ruth Shopped Here

From the book *Babe Ruth and the 1918 Red Sox* by Allan Wood we learn:

> *Babe and Helen Ruth spent the winter of 1917–18 at their farmhouse in Sudbury, Massachusetts. They often took a horse and buggy into the nearby town of Maynard, where Helen would shop and Babe would buy cigars and play pool at the Maynard Smoke Shop, which was owned by Frank*

and Joe Sheridan. The owners' younger brother, nineteen-year-old Ralph Sheridan, had followed the Red Sox since 1908, and he recognized Ruth the first time he walked into the store.

This raises the question: Why was the young Boston Red Sox pitcher living in Sudbury? First, this was not the Dutton Road farmhouse that Babe bought in 1922, when he was already a star for the Yankees. Rather, the story goes that a couple of his teammates on the Red Sox had invited him to visit Sudbury, where they would rent cabins to fish and hunt. For the winter of 1917–18, Ruth rented a modest waterfront cottage near the end of Butler Road (which has since burned down). Maynard was the closest place to go shopping and also to drink, play pool and otherwise carouse.

Ruth was well off at the time but not rich. He was twenty-two years old and had been paid $5,000 for the 1917 season. In today's inflation-adjusted dollars, that would have been approximately $90,000. Baseball in the era before radio or television broadcasting, and all the associated advertising, was America's pastime, but no one got rich.

Babe in Red Sox uniform, 1919. *Library of Congress.*

This story is not complete without a connection to the legend of Babe Ruth's piano. Again, Ralph Sheridan's reminisces, as recounted by Allan Wood:

> *Several times that winter, Ruth invited young men and kids from the area out to his house. Ralph Sheridan worked in a nearby woolen mill and on the weekends, he and some friends, all teenagers, would walk from Maynard, about one mile, across Willis Pond to Ruth's farm. Babe and Helen were often out playing in the snow when Sheridan and his friends came by.*

Sheridan recalled that he and his friends would play outside with Ruth. When they got cold, Helen Ruth invited the boys into the cottage and served them hot cocoa and cookies. "Mrs. Ruth would play the piano and we would all sing along, including the Babe," wrote Sheridan. "He loved kids and always liked to have them around. And, always when we would leave, he would say, 'Come over again and bring the gang.' We were thrilled to be with him."

So how did that piano supposedly end up in Willis Pond? As one version of the story goes, a daytime gathering at the house got overcrowded—the cottage being only twenty by fifty feet—so Ruth and others pushed the piano down the hill and out onto the ice. There, they continued the party complete with singing and dancing while Helen played the piano. When it was time to move the piano back, it was too heavy to push up the hill. So, the Babe simply left the instrument on the ice, where it eventually sank to the bottom.

Kevin Kennedy, a resident of Sudbury, has been searching for the piano for many years. Teams of expert divers have been in the pond more than once. In 2010, a group of divers pulled out pieces of wood, possibly white oak, that piano expert David Sanderson, of Sanderson Piano in Littleton, believed was the veneer of an old upright piano. But as of mid-2014, there was no additional news.

Babe Ruth Drank Here?

Initially, lore of Babe Ruth drinking or otherwise carousing in Maynard appeared to be just that. A few neighboring town waterholes—such as the Dudley Chateau in Wayland—claim to have been speakeasies frequented by Ruth back in the day. The timing would have been in the early 1920s—i.e., after national Prohibition was in effect. What is missing from this story is confirmation of sites within Maynard that were serving booze before or during Prohibition. The two oldest extant bars—the Pleasant Café and Stretch's Tavern (now Morey's) —both postdate the end of Prohibition.

Babe Ruth could have been buying illegally in Maynard and drinking at his Sudbury estate just two miles away. When he bought the farmhouse in 1922, it included a simple cabin on Willis Pond about a half mile from the house. Babe and his friends could head out there for an evening of drinking, card playing and whatnot without disturbing his wife and daughter in the farmhouse. His name for the cabin was "Ihatetoquitit" (I hate to quit it).

A quote often attributed to Babe Ruth, but in fact the work of current-day comic writer Jack Handey: "Sometimes when I reflect on all the beer I drink, I feel ashamed. Then I look into the glass and think about the workers in the brewery and all of their hopes and dreams. If I didn't drink this beer, they might be out of work and their dreams would be shattered. I think, 'It is better to drink this beer and let their dreams come true than be selfish and worry about my liver.'"

On the other hand, this one appears to be true Ruth: "I learned early to drink beer, wine and whiskey. And I think I was about five when I first chewed tobacco."

The Maynard Smoke Shop, east end of the building at 100 Main Street, photo taken about seven years before Babe Ruth started frequenting the joint. Courtesy of Maynard Historical Society.

First appearances were that Ruth was not drinking during his Red Sox years. In Ralph Sheridan's reminisces about visiting Ruth's cabin on Willis Pond, he said he never saw Ruth drink, nor did he see any alcohol in the house. Babe Ruth spent mid-1914 through 1919 with the Red Sox, initially as a pitcher, but by the end he was pitching less and putting in more time as an outfielder. He was sold to the Yankees before the start of the 1920 season.

After two years of Ruth's successes and shenanigans in New York, Colonel Jacob Ruppert, the owner of the Yankees, attempted to curtail Babe's drinking and partying. Thus came this addendum to the contract signed in late 1922:

> *It is understood and agreed by and between the parties hereto that the regulation set forth shall be construed to mean among other things, that the player shall at all times during the term of this contract ($52,000/year) and throughout the years 1922, 1923 and 1924, and the years 1925 and 1926 if this contract is renewed for such years, refrain and abstain entirely from the use of intoxicating liquors and that he shall not during the training and playing season in each year stay up later than 1 o'clock a.m. on any day without the permission and consent of the Club's manager.*

This appears to have been the first morals clause for a professional athlete. Ruppert may have hoped that the Sultan of Swat would also curtail his compulsive womanizing but did not try to get that into the contract. Supposedly, at the time of that meeting, the Babe told Ruppert: "I'll promise to go easier on drinking and to get to bed earlier, but not for you, $50,000 or $250,000 will I give up women. They're too much fun."

While a Yankee, Ruth and his wife made one more stab at reconciling. He returned to Massachusetts, bought the farmhouse and farm at 558 Dutton Road in Sudbury and took up the public image of a gentleman farmer living the good, clean life in the country with his wife and their adopted daughter. Babe was in residence in the winter of 1922–23. After that, his wife continued to reside in Sudbury or elsewhere in the Boston area, but Babe was mostly in New York. They formalized their separation (not a divorce) in 1925, and she sold the house in 1926. Mrs. Ruth died in a house fire in 1929. Babe Ruth remarried and remained married until his death in 1948.

After this column appeared in Maynard's newspaper, I got a phone call from Bob Merriam, Maynard High School class of 1962, with stories about how his grandparents, Niilo and Saimi Hirvonen, knew all about Babe Ruth's drinking in Maynard. According to Bob, during the time when Ruth was still with the Red Sox (and liquor was still legal), Babe would show up at the bar at Bughouse Corner with a big roll of cash in his pocket, slap it on the bar and tell the bartender, "Everyone drinks on Babe Ruth." Not only was he buying, but he also insisted that everyone stay until the bar closed because he liked being around lots of people. He would have been in his early twenties at the time.

Bughouse Corner was a nickname for the intersection of Waltham and Parker, possibly due to speechifying socialists, and came to apply to the bar also. The latter was a low-key, smoke-filled drinking haunt for workers coming off shift at the woolen mill. More than one night, Ruth was too drunk to drive the two miles back to Sudbury (where his wife was home alone in the remote cabin on Willis Pond). Instead, Niilo—himself being a drinking man—saw no problem with inviting Babe Ruth back to his place, where Ruth would sleep it off on the living room floor.

As Bob Merriam told it, "When I was growing up, my grandfather was proud that he had known Babe Ruth, but my grandmother had nothing kind to say." What he heard from her: "'That man would wake up in the night and go outside and pee off the porch instead of using the bathroom.'" When Bob asked his grandfather if this was true, the diplomatic answer was: "Your grandmother has a good memory."

Another story about the Babe and urination is not as well documented. As the story goes, he was an avid golfer and at times played the Stowaway Golf Course (in Stow). When he did, he had, on occasion, stepped into the woods to relieve himself. Some players joke that they might be wetting the same spot honored by Ruth, ninety years ago.

Sid's Airport

Start with a Google search on Maynard, Massachusetts. Select the Maps option. Zoom in a couple of clicks. Drag the map so that it is centered on the west side of town, just north of Summer Street. You will see a designation: "Sid's Airport." A switch to satellite view will confirm a grassy airstrip. At this point, say to yourself, "Really?" Next time you are driving west on Summer Street, remember to glance to the right two houses after passing Durant Avenue on the right. Voila! Sid's Airport.

Sidney H. Mason created his backyard airstrip in 1948 (the same year Orville Wright died). Sid was twenty-eight at the time and an army veteran. He and three friends bought a used Luscombe 1946 8A in 1947 for $1,000.

The plane was a two-seater with an all-aluminum body and wings powered by a sixty-five-horsepower engine. The airstrip land was carved out of what had been an extensive Mason family farm that dated back to at least 1875. In fact, back in the farm days, the family had two runways, and many of the pilots in Maynard and nearby towns kept their planes there.

Sid was still flying in the left-hand (pilot's) seat as late as 1997, at age seventy-nine. A few years before he gave up flying, he had switched over to a 1955 Cessna that needed a bit more runway than his private airstrip provided, so he started flying from Stow's Minute Man Air Field. Meanwhile, Sid's son—Jack Mason—had taken up his father's hobby while still in his teens, earned his pilot's license and was flying a Vector Ultralight in and out of the backyard. This meant that their landing strip continued to be an active, FAA-numbered airstrip (MA52). Sid also soloed the ultralight now and then.

Run the timeline forward to 2012, and Jack Mason had just become the proud owner of a 1946 Luscombe 8E (a model with a bit more horsepower than his dad's old plane). He won the plane in a lottery. By choosing a propeller that maximizes takeoff and climbing power, he has a vintage but modernized plane that can be flown in and out of the landing strip behind his house. Thus, while the plane lives at Stow's airport, Jack can start a

Sidney Mason poses with his wife, Susan, in front of his beloved 1946 Luscombe, on the landing strip behind his house. *Courtesy of Jack Mason.*

voyage from there, stop home for lunch and then head out again…or just step out the back door and into an ultralight.

Sid Mason passed on to the big airport in the sky in 2005. His life-long love affair with the air is memorialized by his tombstone, as it portrays his Luscombe in flight, with the plane's registration number N72025 on the side.

One interesting perspective on the history of flight was that early aviators thought it would put an end to war. In Orville Wright's own words, from a 1917 letter: "When my brother and I built and flew the first man-carrying flying machine, we thought we were introducing into the world an invention which would make further wars practically impossible. We thought governments would realize the impossibility of winning by surprise attacks, and that no country would enter into war with another of equal size when it knew that it would have to win by simply wearing out the enemy."

Orville had a rueful but still optimistic opinion after that war ended: "The aeroplane has made war so terrible that I do not believe any country will again care to start a war." However, by 1946, having lived long enough to witness a second world war, the invention of jet airplanes and the dropping of atomic bombs, he was resigned to his invention being just one more tool of war.

Women at Digital Equipment Corporation

October 10, 1957: A short item on the third page of the *Maynard News* mentioned that Kenneth H. Olsen and Harlan E. Anderson had formed a new electronics company named Digital Equipment Corporation. Both of them had been employees at MIT's Lincoln Laboratory before striking out on their own. Ken was thirty-one and Harlan twenty-eight. They started with 8,680 square feet of space, rented for $3,600 a year.

For the first three years, they were producing electronic test modules for engineering laboratories and in the meantime working on Phase II of their plan: Digital's first computer, to be named the PDP-1. By October 1961, the company had grown to 265 employees. In time, Digital made Maynard the "mini-computer capital of the world."

Olsen was a big believer in numbers. Employees were assigned consecutive numbers based on order of hire, later becoming their badge numbers. Ken was #1. Harlan was #2. The first two women hired were Alma E. Pontz, #5, and Gloria Porrazzo, #6.

Women were not rare at Digital. From perusing a list of the first one hundred full-time employees, thirty-six were women. Years later, the main reasons Olsen gave for locating in Maynard were low rent and a local workforce with lots of factory experience. Many of the women were walk-to-work Maynardites who had worked in the same buildings in the woolen mill era, ten to twenty years back. The newly refurbished work area was clean, quiet and well lit, although hot during the summers, as no air conditioning was installed until around 1970. Throughout the buildings, summer weather meant lanolin from the old wool-processing days dripping down the walls or from the ceilings above.

Alma E. Pontz was the first woman hired. According to her 2013 obituary, she had already put in twenty-four years in the wool business before being hired by Olsen as the first administrative assistant and thus was more than a decade older than her bosses. She stayed with DEC until she retired twenty-one years later. Gloria Porrazzo was the first woman hired to work in assembling the Laboratory Modules and Systems Modules. These products allowed Digital to be profitable from its first year onward. According to plant manager Peter Koch, Porrazzo stayed with the company for twenty-five years, rising to the level of production manager. The fifty to sixty women who worked for her in assembly were informally known as "Gloria's Girls." They were responsible for inserting electronic components into circuit boards, welding and quality control. Ken Olsen was known to drop in for coffee and a chat with Gloria to keep abreast of any production problems.

Digital was not averse to hiring women with technical expertise, but some of the customers had a hard time adapting. Barbara Stephenson, MIT graduate, employee #71, was hired the second year. As posted at www. computerhistory.org: "I was the first woman engineer at DEC. Customers would call for an applications engineer. They would say, 'I want to speak with an engineer,' and I would reply, 'I'm an engineer,' and they would say, 'No, I want to speak with a real engineer.' I developed this patter: 'Well, tell me about the application you have in mind. We have three lines of modules ranging from five to ten megacycles and...' The line would go dead for a moment and then I'd hear, 'Hey Joe, guess what, I've got a...woman... engineer on the phone!'"

Women were promoted from within. Maynard resident Angela Cossette was hired as an administrative assistant in 1963 in support for DEC User's Society. DECUS provided a pre-Internet forum for computer users to exchange technical information and user-developed software. Cossette moved up to becoming the company's first female manager, in time with as many as one hundred people reporting to her. In her own words, "Digital became very aggressive about giving women the opportunity to grow in their careers and making it possible for them to move into key positions." Cossette retired in 1992.

Her comment reflected Digital's self-realization that it had a problem with its history of male-dominated culture. A Core Groups program was started in 1977, evolving into the "Valuing Differences" philosophy in 1984. The stated goal was for the company and its employees to pay attention to differences of individuals and groups, to be comfortable with those differences and to use those differences as assets to the company's productivity.

Digital peaked in late 1989 or early 1990 with more than 120,000 employees worldwide and ambitions to overtake IBM. Instead, overly fast growth combined with a series of missteps led to a precipitous decline that ended with a sale to Compaq, which in turn was bought by Hewlett-Packard.

Fleepo the Clown, aka Philip Bohunicky

November 2014 marked ten years since Philip W. Bohunicky, aka "Fleepo the Clown," passed away, a month shy of his eighty-fifth birthday. Phil had been a fixture in Maynard's parades and celebrations for close to forty years. He, as have others, qualified for the honorary title "Mr. Maynard" in his time.

Phil wrote up part of his life's story for the Maynard Historical Society shortly before he died. As he told it, he began sponsoring and coordinating Maynard's Christmas parade in 1966 because of an event from his youth. His early memories were of growing up in a Catholic orphanage. He described a snowy winter evening when the nuns told the boys that after evening prayers they were to put on their winter outfits. They walked to the center of town, where he heard a small band playing "Jingle Bells," and everyone joined in to sing Christmas carols.

In his own words, "All of a sudden a huge red fire engine appeared around the corner with its sirens and horns blasting away. Standing in the back of the fire engine was a huge Santa Claus waving and yelling, 'Merry Christmas, merry Christmas! Ho, ho, ho!' As Santa faded slowly in the distance, I was mesmerized, and to this day, oh-so-long, long after, I never forgot when I first saw Santa Claus when I was only six years old and living in the orphanage."

In addition to starting the Maynard Christmas Parade tradition, behind the scenes he also personally covered much of the cost of putting on the event, a responsibility since taken on by the Rotary Club. Phil also organized the annual Easter Egg Hunt at Crowe Park and helped provide entertainment at the Fourth of July carnivals at the same location. At many events, he was joined by his children, and others in the seven-to-ten age range, who performed as the Happy Toe Square Dancers.

Phil's main alter ego was Fleepo the Clown, but he also put in appearances at children's and charity events as Grandpa Fleepo or Harmonica Phil. Many Maynardites remember Fleepo on WAVM's *The Fleepo Show*; or in costume, on roller skates, handing out lollipops; or seeing him drive by—in costume, on his way to an event—with a very, very large stuffed panda in the car as his sidekick. His license plate read FLEEPO. One story that made local news in April 1990 was that Fleepo was hatjacked of his signature antique top hat at the Easter Egg event. Sadly, the hat was never recovered.

As for how his clown name came to be: Philip clown-apprenticed for years with Chris Sclarppia, who went by the name "Bozo" (not the famous Bozo). Chris took the French pronunciation of Phil's name—think "Fe-leep"—and from there mutated it to "Fleepo."

Out of costume, Bohunicky put in uncounted hours supporting Little League baseball, T-ball and the water safety swim program conducted at Lake Boon. He had served in the Army Medical Corps in Europe during World War II and appeared in uniform at Memorial Day and Veterans Day remembrances. His postwar career was as an electronics technician at MIT's Lincoln Labs in Lexington. Bohunicky died on Veterans Day 2004.

Little is known about Bohunicky's family history. One source mentions both of his parents dying when he was an infant, and with no other family member to take him in, he ended up at St. John's Catholic Orphanage in Utica, New York, until he was eleven and then lived with a series of foster families. His good luck was the last family insisting he finish high school and then the GI Bill putting him through Massachusetts Trade School.

Phil's contributions to town spirit continue to be remembered. Each year, the Philip Bohunicky Humanitarian Award is presented at the WAVM banquet to a member of the town who exemplifies the same type of dedication to his or her community.

7

TWENTY-FIRST CENTURY

I n reply to the question "What is history?" my answer is "Everything up until this morning's cup of coffee." Maynard's older history is well-served by books recounting how the land was acquired from Native Americans or what brought the various immigrant groups here, but some space needs to be dedicated to the recent memory of what is happening now, else it pass unrecorded and forgotten.

The Bridges of Maynard

The oldest bridge in Maynard—as in the age of the current span—is closing in on its centennial year. The oldest bridge site is a different story. A modern bridge carries White Pond Road across the Assabet River at the Stow–Maynard border. Documents in the archives of the Sudbury Historical Society record the first bridge at this site as built in 1716. The road over the original bridge—New Lancaster Road—connected Sudbury to Stow and was part of the principal stagecoach route from Boston to Lancaster.

In 1800, this was known as Dr. Wood's Bridge. Jonathan Wood Jr. (1761–1822) was a doctor of medicine. His name became attached to the bridge because patients coming north from Sudbury had to cross it to see him. Years later, it became known as Russell's Bridge, for reasons no longer known to local historians.

White Pond Road Bridge (2007) is on the site of the first bridge to span the Assabet River (1716).

Until 1816 this was the only bridge over the Assabet within what are now Maynard's borders. Some of the other spots were fords—shallow places where a horse and wagon could cross. High water made these sites temporarily impassable.

As seen in the table on page 111, four bridges pre-dated the arrival of Amory Maynard in 1846. In addition to Dr. Wood's Bridge, the Post Road (now Route 117) crossing was built in 1816, as was a bridge to Jewel's Mill. What is now the Waltham Street Bridge was once known as the Paper Mill Bridge, as it was adjacent to a paper mill built around 1820.

Today's in-town bridge count is ten: seven road bridges and one footbridge spanning the Assabet, plus two over the canal that had been excavated as part of Amory's project to channel water from the new dam to the new millpond.

Missing from that count are two long-gone railroad bridges—one over the Assabet at the site of the Tobin Park footbridge, removed in 1980, and the other over the canal, southwest of where Mill Street meets Route 117.

Construction methods of the post-colonial era were simple: build stone piers at either end, span the gap with logs and plank the top. For a

Plaque on the Main Street Bridge dedicating the bridge to the memory of the women and men who served in the Civil, Spanish-American and World Wars.

wider river, add a central stone pier. Repair often meant just replanking. Stone and mortar bridges such as the Mill Street Bridge cost more to construct but were stronger and longer lasting. Stone was superseded by steel; in 1872, both Main Street and Walnut Street were newly spanned by steel bridges.

The science of reinforcing concrete with steel rods made major advances in the early twentieth century and is reflected in the spate of local bridges built in the 1920s. Unfortunately, these bridges have surpassed expected lifespan. Ages shown in table are for 1914. Order is date of first bridge at each site.

The Waltham Street bridge had a serious case of the concrete crumbles before the current replacement project began, which brings us back to

Table V
BRIDGES IN ORDER OF CONSTRUCTION OF FIRST BRIDGE AT EACH SITE

BRIDGE NAME	FIRST	INTERIM	CURRENT	AGE	MATERIAL
White Pond Road	1716	1800, 1929	2007	7	Reinforced concrete
Route 117	1816	????	1922	92	Reinforced concrete
Mill Street	1816	????	1922	92	Mortar and stone
Waltham Street	1840	1928	2013	1	Reinforced concrete
Route 117 (canal)	1846	-----	1941	73	Reinforced concrete
Main Street	1849	1872, 1901	1922	92	Reinforced concrete
Sudbury Road (canal)	1855	1915, 1955	2002	12	Reinforced concrete
Walnut Street	1865	1872	1922	92	Reinforced concrete
Florida Road	1915	-----	1915	99	Reinforced concrete
Tobin Park (footbridge)	????	1989	1989	25	Wood

the oldest existing bridge: Florida Road. This once-handsome bridge is in disrepair. It also has narrow lanes and poor sight lines. However, it is not yet scheduled for replacement. The next major bridge in the Massachusetts Department of Transportation queue is the Main Street Bridge, tentatively planned to start in 2019, which will bring to four the count of twenty-first-century replacements.

What This Town Needs Is a Good Hotel

Before Maynard was Maynard, there were a few inns on the stagecoach line that ran through what was then the northwest end of Sudbury and is now Maynard's part of the Assabet River National Wildlife Refuge. Rice Tavern stood for nearly one hundred years, to 1815. The one-time Levi Smith house was converted to a tavern and did stagecoach and traveler duty from 1816 to 1848.

With the building of Maynard's and Knight's woolen mill in 1846 came the need for worker housing: boardinghouses. These had furnished rooms and were rented to workers by the week or month. Most were owned by either the mill or members of the Maynard family. Some were substantial—the Middlesex & Assabet House, at the site now occupied by the post office, had thirty-nine rooms to let at twenty-five dollars a month. Some of Maynard's current rental housing was once boardinghouses.

The first hotel was Glendale House, built on Summer Street in 1867. This became the Maynard Hotel, operating under that name until it burned on January 29, 1921. The Town of Maynard bought the land and on November 15, 1925, dedicated the Memorial Park war monuments on the site of the hotel building.

Maple House opened for business in 1880. The building was torn down in the 1940s. The site is currently occupied by the Maynard Fire Department. American House, on Harriman Court, was owned and operated by the Loewe family from the 1890s to the early 1920s. Glendale House (the second by that name) opened across Summer Street from the Maynard Hotel in 1901—closing year unknown. And the Somerset Hotel launched at the corner of Main and River Streets in 1908, later doing stints as a grocery store and food co-op. Since 1945, the Pleasant Café has occupied the site. For those keeping count, all this history meant that five hotels were in business at the same time from around 1910 to 1920. From this peak, the numbers declined until after World War II there were none.

After a long period with no hotels within town borders, Leon Christian opened the Maynard Motel on Route 62 in 1962, with fourteen rooms to let. The one-story building straddled the Maynard–Acton border. A Wendy's restaurant now occupies part of the site. A town business directory from 1989 listed the motel as still in operation, and one resident confirmed visiting family staying there in 1990. It appears the motel closed shortly after that.

As for why Maynard does not currently have a hotel or motel, that's a bit of a mystery. Aside from a handful of Airbnb rentals and bed-and-breakfast operations, the closest accommodation is a Best Western Plus in Concord, 4.8 miles from downtown Maynard. Beyond that, one needs to be willing to travel 7.0 to 10.0 miles away from Maynard in order to find other franchise brand hotels in Hudson, Boxborough, Westford, Marlborough, Framingham, Natick, Lexington and Waltham. Alternatively, historic accommodations are offered by the Colonial Inn in Concord and Longfellow's Wayside Inn in Sudbury.

What would it take to open an upscale hotel in Maynard? Perhaps as much as $10 million, either for conversion of an existing mill building or new construction, plus a hotel business plan that makes economic sense. After all, there are already close to two thousand hotel or motel rooms within ten miles of downtown Maynard—just none in town (or in Stow, or Acton or north Sudbury). Still, it's fun to imagine a hotel overlooking the millpond, nightclub on the roof, brewpub on the first floor and live music.

Oldest Restaurant

As of 2014, Stow was home to nine food establishments, for a ratio of one per every 730 residents. Maynard, with a population not quite twice that of Stow, offered twenty-five restaurants and thus a restaurant ratio close to one per every 405 residents. Acton and Sudbury fell somewhere in between for restaurants per capita.

Deciding whether to open a restaurant, and where, is as much an art as it is a science. The rule of thumb is that 25 percent of newly opened restaurants will close or change owners in the first year. Cumulatively, the total is roughly 50 percent by the end of the third year. The Peyton's RiversEdge site on Powder Mill Road went through some fast-paced iterations—Malcolm's Steakhouse, Christopher's, JoJo's West and Johnny Ray's Ultimate—before its last incarnation (which closed in January 2014).

"Where" is always an interesting question. Being away from other restaurants might, in theory, be considered a plus, but experience shows that being near other restaurants works out better.

Maynard has been a restaurant nexus for a long time. Business directories from the 1930s and 1940s list fifteen to twenty restaurants. Many were at the same sites as today's litany but with different names. Among the lost: Allen's Café, Millstream Lunch, Muzzey's, Paul's Bakery, Priest's Café, Riley's Tavern, Russo's Restaurant, Twin Tree Inn and White's Diner.

One nice thing about today's proximity of all the dining and drinking establishments in Maynard is that you can park the car and have an old-fashioned pub crawl. In May 2013, the liquid establishments of Maynard cepebrated…celebraded…celebrated…C-E-L-E-B-R-A-T-E-D their first annual pub crawl organized to raise funds for Remembering Maynard's Own. RMO conducts fundraising events to help cover what Maynard High School students need to pay for school activities' participation fees. In doing so, these MHS grads remember and honor deceased classmates, family members and friends. Pub crawls honoring veterans are also now an annual event.

The 2013 crawl included Cast Iron Kitchen (since closed), River Rock Grill, Blue Coyote, China Ruby, Halfway Café, Pleasant Café and Morey's Tavern, with a finale at the Elk's Lodge. Interestingly, all but China Ruby and Pleasant Café are twenty-first-century names for sites that had prior histories as oases of alcohol. River Rock was the Sit'n Bull, and Blue Coyote was Amory's Pub.

Think quick—what is Maynard's oldest restaurant (defined as same site, same name)? Erikson's Ice Cream recently turned seventy-six, but not as a

Researching this article led to a concern that the oldest restaurant in town might be McDonald's, as the franchise opened in 1978, but as it turned out, the Pleasant Café was older by several decades.

restaurant. Morey's Tavern is disqualified because of a name change, as it was Stretch's Tavern (1937–2005) before the current incarnation.

The winner is Pleasant Café at 36 Main Street. Per its website: "Serving cold beer since 1945." According to a walking tour compiled by the Maynard Historical Commission, the building was constructed around 1899. Earlier tenants were the Somerset Hotel, Cleary & Williams Dry Goods and Millinery, Jersey Butter Company, Arena & Sons Grocery and the Royal Café. The Pleasant Café, also known as the PC, actually dates further back than 1945. The town's 1936 business directory lists an establishment by that name at a different address. The current owners confirm that the family business opened at 157½ Main Street around 1934–35, closed for World War II and then reopened at the current site after the war. This makes the PC not just Maynard's oldest restaurant but also one of a small handful of local businesses owned and operated by the same family for more than seventy years.

The Town Dump, Repurposed

Maynard stinks. At least according to Sudbury, or the northernmost residents of Sudbury whose property was close to Maynard's town dump around 1958. Maynard's close-by residents had the same complaint.

At that time, Maynard's landfill operation was an open pit next to Waltham Street, the land rented from the Boeske family that had been one side of their still active gravel pit. Townspeople brought their own garbage to the town dump, open six days a week (closed Mondays). The litany of complaints included bad smells and also smoke, ash and embers from intentional, town-managed trash burning. A few times a year, the Town of Maynard would level the trash heaps with a bulldozer and add a layer of dirt and gravel, but town records show that there was still call for a chemical control program to kill rats and flies.

Not documented in the annual reports, but confirmed in talks with longtime residents, is that one local pastime was going to the dump to shoot rats. Ah, moonlit evenings; the smell, smoke and flickering light of still-smoldering garbage; a high-powered flashlight; a .22 rifle; and a box of rimfire ammo. Beer optional.

According to Walter Sokolowski, who had been with the town's Department of Public Works for more than forty years, Maynard's open dump era ended soon after the 1963 order to all towns by the Massachusetts State Department of Health to stop burning trash and to convert to sanitary landfill (meaning that new trash was covered with dirt). As part of the transition, Maynard had to switch to garbage truck pickup rather than resident dumping. The town also started thinking about what to do after the existing site reached capacity. One new site under consideration was the wetlands west of the high school, with the idea that it could later be capped and used as a playground.

Landfill at Waltham Street continued until 1980, by which time the level had risen to above that of the road. By then, the land had become property of the town, and the Massachusetts Department of Environmental Protection (MassDEP) had gotten involved in regulating waste management. Retired dumps needed methane gas venting and monitoring of local ground water to make sure that environmental pollutants were not moving through the soil to nearby streams, ponds and wells. Maynard's landfill closed in 1980; was capped with soil, sand and clay in 1988; and certified closed by MassDEP in 1995.

Around 2009, the Town of Maynard began to explore installing a solar panel array on the old dump site. The proposal was approved at town meeting in 2010 and subsequently approved by MassDEP in the fall of

The solar panel array started generating power in 2013.

2012. Construction started that December. The completed solar panel array went active in 2013, putting Maynard among the initial fifteen such landfill conversion facilities to become operative in Massachusetts.

All told, the town owns about thirteen acres of land adjacent to Waltham Street, of which six to seven acres was dump, and now just under five acres are covered by solar panels. The installation is described as a 1.2-megawatt solar photovoltaic array of approximately five thousand panels mounted on concrete blocks, those resting on gravel. Nothing penetrates the clay layer used to cap the old landfill. The panels are static (do not tip or turn) and are set to face southwest to maximize sunlight.

Maynard did not pay for construction. Electricity generated by the panels goes into the regional grid; in return, the operating company pays the town an annual fee of about $75,000. The lease runs for twenty years with an option for a ten-year extension, at the end of which the operator is responsible for removing all parts of system.

The solar array is fenced on all sides. An adjoining area of under one-half acre is also fenced as a dog park or, in dog parlance, an off-leash recreation area. The dog park is outside the footprint of the original dump, so no amount of dog digging will ever get down to old trash. Dogs will have an opportunity to socialize with other dogs. (Owners can socialize, too.) There is some space for parking. The facility is the culmination of a multi-year effort by members of MayDOG, which had originally hoped for a much larger fraction of the dump to be repurposed for dogs:

"Dump Haiku"
Rain-sodden garbage
Fire, smoke, smells, rats and flies
Now dog run and sun.

ArtSpace and Acme Theater

Art does not pay. Or to be exact, art does not pay much, which is why artists are often looking at less than ideal studio or living space to encamp. In cities, these distressed areas are often semi-abandoned, run-down, industrial spaces. And sadly, history tells us that trailblazing artists are followed by hipsters, who are followed by trendy retail businesses and restaurants, and then the cool money pours in—and you have Brooklyn.

Fifteen years ago, the Town of Maynard decided to explore the idea of supporting the presence of artists in its midst. The catalyst was deciding what to do with a surplus school. Construction of Fowler Middle School on the south side of town meant that the old complex on Summer Street, parts dating back to 1916, would stand empty. Maynard already had the bad example of an empty ex-school with the Roosevelt School building, which was progressively decaying since closing in 1956 (finally, phoenix-like, resurrected as Maynard Public Library in 2006).

Ideas for what to do with the old Fowler school had come from two directions. First, the town voted to appoint a Fowler School Building Reuse Committee in 1996. Second, a handful of local artists, self-named Assabet River Artists Association (ARAA), had begun an effort to create a group identity. Among these were Darthea Cross, Erik Hansen, Bruce Lucier and Sarah Matias. ARAA had business cards printed and a few group shows. Meanwhile, in 1999, the reuse committee reached a conclusion that the only realistic plan was to lease the space to a nonprofit arts/cultural group.

The official transfer of the building to ArtSpace, Inc., took place in January 2001. Today, ArtSpace provides forty-three studio spaces for seventy-five artists (some share). Demand remains high, with perhaps one or two studios becoming available each year. Rent for the artists is about

The building looks like a school because it was a school from 1916 to 2000, housing at different times the high school, middle school and elementary school.

eight dollars per square foot. The money raised pays for a full-time executive director—Jero Nesson—and cover operating costs. The town pays nothing toward operation of ArtSpace, but as it owns the building and charges only a nominal rent, it does not gain any property tax revenue, either.

Key to getting ArtSpace off the ground was hiring Nesson away from his position at Emerson Umbrella, a school-to-studios complex located in Concord. He had been with Emerson for eleven years. Prior to that, he was involved with ArtSpace of Wellesley and before that, Brickbottom in Somerville and the Fort Point Arts Community in Boston. His current role spans the gamut, from promoting the existence of ArtSpace to the public to being a pipe whisperer to the ancient steam heat, plumbing and stormwater drainpipes crisscrossing the building and grounds.

Acme Theater Productions, currently inhabiting basement space at ArtSpace, has a longer history than its host. Acme began in 1992. Prior to 2001, it was a troupe without a home, rehearsing where it could storing props and scenery wherever it could and performing at schools and other public

David Sheppard stands in front of a wall of 8x10s from just a fraction of the Acme Theater productions put on since the troupe moved into the ArtSpace building.

spaces. The troupe took on the slogan "Home of the Misfits" to reflect its can-do (with less) attitude. Despite lack of a permanent space, ATP produced award-winning plays and traveled nationally and even internationally.

David Sheppard, founder and executive director of Acme Theater Productions, has been with ATP since day one. Per the Acme website, he provides the group with vision, creative energy and a commitment to quality and has won numerous director awards. In 2001, Acme formally became a nonprofit corporation and, as such, became eligible for space at ArtSpace. All hands, including a few hammered thumbs, converted the ex-school's woodshop into a seventy-seat theater. Sheppard characterized their space as "dark, downstairs—and much loved."

And so the experiment succeeded. ArtSpace continues to be fully occupied with artists, some in place since the start, and has a waiting list of applicants. Priority is given to Maynard residents. Many of the studios are open to the public every second Saturday of every month. The ArtSpace Gallery is a wonderful exhibition space presenting new and important contemporary art by both in-house and nationally known artists. All this offers a wonderful—and free—opportunity to see art, chat with artists and buy their art.

A Cleaner River: The Assabet Transformed

In its natural state, the Assabet was a glorious little river, but historically it took awhile to settle on a name. Old maps show Assabeth, Asabet, Elizbeth, Elizabet…all thought to be Anglicized versions of an Algonquin Indian name. Nathaniel Hawthorne wrote: "Rowing our boat against the current, between wide meadows, we turn aside into the Assabeth. A more lovely stream than this, for a mile above its junction with the Concord, has never flowed on earth."

Given its modest length and modest volume, the Assabet was an extremely "worked" river, meaning that little remains of its original natural state. From the headwaters, where a dam ensures less flow in times of flood and more flow in times of drought, to the conflux thirty-one miles and 220 feet lower in elevation where it merges with the Sudbury River to become the Concord River, the Assabet had powered eight mills, had its high-water rampages hobbled by flood control dams, suffered channeling between restraining walls through the center of Hudson and Maynard, lost water to our various usages and gained water back from our numerous waste streams.

From Thoreau's journal entry in 1859: "So completely emasculated and demoralized is our river that it is even made to observe the Christian Sabbath…for then the river runs lowest owing to the factory and mill gates being shut. Not only the operatives make the Sunday a day of rest but the river too, to some extent, so that the very fishes feel the influence…of man's religion." His point here is that natural flow was stopped at the end of Saturday's workday so as to back up as much water as possible before work started again Monday morning.

The Assabet was also an extremely polluted river. As Ann Zwinger wrote in *A Conscious Stillness* (1982), "The reach above the Powder Mill Dam is closed by joint action of the Maynard and Acton Boards of Health." She added, "The river smell is nauseating, reeking like an unpumped-out campground outhouse times ten."

By then, the issue was no longer industrial pollution left over from the mills that had dotted the Assabet River and its tributaries. Rather, the smells emanated from rotting of bacteria, algae and water plants such as duckweed—the consequence of eutrophic growth promoted by the excesses of phosphorus and nitrogen entering the water from wastewater treatment plants (WWTPs). Five of these return cleaned water to the Assabet. Their combined volume is so great that in the low-flow months of summer, most of the water in the river is processed water. Surface water run-off of fertilizer from farms, golf courses and lawns also contributes unwanted nutrients, as does untreated stormwater from roads and parking lots.

Until quite recently, the limits on phosphorus content of processed water were not stringent enough to lower the rampant warm weather plant growth. But starting in 2009 and completed in 2014, all of the WWTPs on the Assabet River now meet higher standards. Mid-summer phosphorus content in the river has been reduced from 0.4 to 0.8 milligrams per liter to about 0.1 milligrams per liter. A target is to get below 0.025 milligrams per liter. Large amounts of sediment trapped behind dams harbor reserves of phosphorus and nitrogen, thus slowing the trend to a healthier river, but over time, the water quality will continue to improve.

All this focus on plant growth is not to say that local rivers had not suffered from industrial insult. Back in the day, wool arrived in Maynard unwashed. Cleaning it at the factory meant all the lanolin, dirt, urine and feces matted into the fleece ended up in the river, along with the chemical dyes and whatever. Children frolicked in the river behind the Main Street School (where town hall is now) but not downstream of the mill.

One saving grace—the Assabet did not suffer the extensive mercury dumping that still haunts the Sudbury River. From 1917 to 1978, the Nyanza Color & Chemical Company operated a textile dye manufacturing factory in Ashland. Wastewater entered the Sudbury River via a tributary named Chemical Brook (how apt). The Environmental Protection Agency estimates that forty-five to fifty-seven metric tons of mercury were released into the Sudbury River. Other contaminants included chromium, arsenic, lead and carcinogenic chemicals. The current advisory: "The general public should not consume any fish from this water body."

Solid waste trash also contributed to the Assabet's lack of ambiance. In Maynard alone, decades of annual river cleanups have been organized by OARS, the watershed organization for the Assabet, Sudbury and Concord Rivers. OARS has removed more than one thousand car and truck tires, tons of metal scrap and hundreds upon hundreds of pounds of broken glass. Intact glass bottles from fifty to sixty years ago have come out of the river. Ditto televisions, bicycles, shopping carts and beer cans. A saving grace here is that cleaning up the river appears contagious so that each year less new trash goes into the river.

OARS (watershed organization for the Assabet, Sudbury and Concord Rivers) has been conducting annual cleanups since 1984. This haul came out of the Assabet River in 2012.

You Know You're from Maynard...

...if you remember twenty or more of the following: 17 Summer Restaurant, 51 Main Street Restaurant, A&P supermarket, the Alchemist Health Foods, Allen's Café, Alphonse's Powder Mill Restaurant, Amory's, Anderson Ford, Army & Navy Surplus Store, Assabet Institute for Savings, Avalon Restaurant, the railroad station (passenger trains to Boston until 1958), Bacharach's Grocery, Batley & Sons Florists, Beacon Santa Telethons, Bikeworx motorcycle shop, Boeske's gas station, getting driving lessons from Bug-eyed Bob...

Brick Oven Pizza, Butler Lumber, Café La Mattina, Carbone's Twin Tree Café, Cast Iron Kitchen, CD Willy's, Center Dance Studio, Ciro's Restaurant, the Clothes Inn, Colonial Theater (movies for nine cents), Copper Kettle Restaurant, the Corner Closet consignment store, Creative Camera, Dennison Manufacturing Company, working for Digital, Donutland (now Babico's), Dunia, Dunn Oil, Easter Egg hunts at Crowe Park, Elizabeth Schnair's newsstand, the Elmwood Street bathhouse and sauna, Erikson's Ice Cream, Factory Outlet, feeding millpond ducks and geese at the Farmers' Market...

Fine Arts Theatre, the fire station horn sounding at 12:10 p.m., Fleepo the Clown (aka Philip Bohunicky), Flipside Records, the flood of August 1955 (Hurricane Diane), Fraternal Order of Eagles, Fred's TV, Geek Boutique, the Gail Shop, GO TIGERS!, Grandmothers' Trunk, Gramps' Garage, Grappa's Restaurant, Gruber Bros. Furniture, the gym at Emerson-Fowler School, Happy Toe Square Dancers, the old high school (and the older old high school), the hurricane of 1938, ice-skating on Cemetery Pond, India Palace, Irene's Stitch-It Shop, JJ Newberry variety store, Jacob's Market, Jimmy's Variety, John J. Tobin ("Mr. Maynard"), Johnson Pharmacy, JoJo's West...

Butler Lumber is one of several multigenerationally owned businesses in Maynard, but the name stems from the business being started on Butler Avenue rather than ever being owned by the Butler family.

Kelly's Bowling Lanes (candlepin, of course), Knights of Columbus, La Petite Auberge, Leapin' Lena appearing in parades, Lovell Bus Lines, M&B Lunch, Malcolm's Steakhouse, Manning Pharmacy, Massa's Bakery, Martin & Doran Funeral Home, the Charles A. Welch Lodge in the Masonic Building, Maydale Beverage Company, Maynard High School bonfires at homecoming, Maynard Motel, Maynard Smoke Shop...

Peeking through the door into the Maynard family crypt, Maynard's centennial celebration, motorcycle charity rides parading through town and ending at the Rod and Gun Club, Mr. Takeout, Murphy & Snyder Printers, Nason Street Spa, New Idea Store, Northern Recording Studio, helping OAR (Organization for the Assabet River) pull tires and other trash out of the river, Oktoberfest fireworks, "Only in Maynard" T-shirts, Oriental Delight, drinks at the PC, Parker Hardware, Parker Street Hall (the Finnish Workingmen's Socialist Society), Patty's Donut Shop, Paul's Bakery...

Peoples Theatre, Peyton's RiversEdge, Prescott Paint, Priest's Café, Quinteros, the Red Door (and Ma), Rickles Cut Rate, Rob Henry's Tavern, Rodoff Shalom Synagogue, Russo's restaurant, St. Casimir's Polish Catholic

The spraypainted mural on the warehouse behind Gruber Bros. Furniture was first created by members of CinderBlockHustle in 2008 and then revised in 2012 with a patriotic theme.

Church, St. George's Episcopal Church, St. John's Finnish Evangelical Lutheran Church, Salamone's, Samuels Studio, Santa arriving for the Christmas parade by helicopter, Screech Owl yearbooks, elementary school trips to the Clock Tower to see the clock…

Sears & Roebuck's catalogue store, Sheehan and White Funeral Home, shooting rats at the town dump, Sid's Airport, drinking Bud Light on Silver Hill, live music at the Sit'n Bull Tavern, skating at Thanksgiving Pond, sledding at the golf course, Sons of Italy, Speedy's Pizza, Stretch's Tavern, T.C Lando's Sub & Pizzeria (lost to a fire in 1998), Taurus Leather Shop, horrible smells from the Taylor mink ranch, Tennis Court Dances, Teresina's vintage clothing, Tobin's Pizza, Town Paint, Tutto's bowling alley and pool hall, Taylor Chevrolet, United Co-op, Victory Market, Vincent's Antiques, W.A. Twombly Funeral Home, when traffic was two ways on Main and Nason Streets, walking the trestle, WAVM, W.B. Case & Sons, Western Auto, Woodrow Wilson School fire (1952), going to a woodsy, Woolworths, and Ye Olde Town House Pub…

Please share this list with people who have moved away from Maynard. Who knows? Maybe they will move back.

BIBLIOGRAPHY

Books

Boothroyd, Paul, and Lewis Halprin. *Assabet Mills, Images of America*. Mount Pleasant, SC: Arcadia, 1999.

———. *Maynard Massachusetts, Images of America*. Mount Pleasant, SC: Arcadia, 1999.

———. *Maynard, Postcard History Series*. Mount Pleasant, SC: Arcadia, 2005.

Earls, Alan R. *Digital Equipment Corporation, Images of America*. Mount Pleasant, SC: Arcadia, 2004.

Gutteridge, William H. *A Brief History of the Town of Maynard, Massachusetts*. Maynard, MA: Town of Maynard, 1921.

Hudson, Alfred. *The Annals of Sudbury, Wayland, and Maynard, Middlesex County, Massachusetts*. N.p.: self-published, 1891.

Lemire, Elise. *Black Walden*. Philadelphia: University of Pennsylvania Press, 2009.

Schein, Edgar H. *DEC Is Dead, Long Live DEC: The Lasting Legacy of Digital Equipment Corporation*. San Francisco: Berrett-Koehler, 2004.

Sheridan, Ralph. *A History of Maynard, 1871–1971*. Maynard, MA: Town of Maynard Historical Committee, 1971.

Voogd, Jan. *Maynard Massachusetts, A House in the Village*. Charleston, SC: The History Press, 2007.

Zwinger, Ann, and Edwin Way Teale. *A Conscious Stillness: Two Naturalists on Thoreau's Rivers*. New York: Harper and Row, 1982.

Websites

Massachusetts Historical Society: http://www.masshist.org
Maynard Historical Society: http://maynardhistory.org
OARS: http://www.oars3rivers.org
Stow Historical Society: http://stowhistoricalsociety.org
Sudbury Historical Society: http://www.sudbury01776.org

ABOUT THE AUTHOR

David A. Mark was born in New York City and grew up in northern New Jersey. He became a reader early but a writer late, as his first book, *Maynard: History and Life Outdoors*, was published after he turned sixty. He and his wife, Jean D'Amico, have lived in Maynard since 2000 in their circa 1870 house. They have a barn with what was a horse stall and a chicken coop, the former now space for David's bicycles, the latter Jean's pottery studio. Both of them are avid gardeners. Prior to moving to Maynard, they had done stints in Chicago and New York.

When not writing, Mark is a consultant—or, as he puts it, a company of one. He wisecracks, "The only problem I have with being self-employed is that when I call in sick, I know I'm lying." Mark has a doctorate in nutritional biochemistry from the Massachusetts Institute of Technology. His consulting business focuses on advising dietary supplement and food companies on the quality of science needed to support their desired health claims.

About the Author

Mark takes frequent breaks from his deskwork to do volunteer maintenance and improvement on the Assabet River Rail Trail and on Maynard's woodland trails. As he puts it, "It's either this or join a gym—and this is free."

Most of the content of this book was written as a column for the *Beacon-Villager* weekly newspaper, serving Maynard and Stow. Mark's first column was published in November 2009. The column count is approaching 170. Columns published subsequent to this book can be viewed at www.maynardlifeoutdoors.com.